BRONTË COUNTRY

HILLSIDE GUIDES - ACROSS THE NORTH & BEYOND

The Uplands of Britain
- **THE HIGH PEAKS OF ENGLAND & WALES**
- **YORKSHIRE DALES, MOORS & FELLS**

Long Distance Walks
- **COAST TO COAST WALK**
- **DALES WAY**
- **CLEVELAND WAY**
- **WESTMORLAND WAY**
- **FURNESS WAY**
- **CUMBERLAND WAY**
- **BRONTE WAY**
- **PENDLE WAY**
- **NIDDERDALE WAY**
- **LADY ANNE'S WAY**
- **TRANS-PENNINE WAY**
- **CALDERDALE WAY**

Hillwalking - Lake District
- **LAKELAND FELLS - SOUTH**
- **LAKELAND FELLS - EAST**
- **LAKELAND FELLS - NORTH**
- **LAKELAND FELLS - WEST**

Circular Walks - Peak District
- **NORTHERN PEAK**
- **EASTERN PEAK**
- **CENTRAL PEAK**
- **SOUTHERN PEAK**
- **WESTERN PEAK**

Circular Walks - Yorkshire Dales
- **HOWGILL FELLS**
- **THREE PEAKS**
- **MALHAMDALE**
- **WHARFEDALE**
- **NIDDERDALE**
- **WENSLEYDALE**
- **SWALEDALE**

Circular Walks - North York Moors
- **WESTERN MOORS**
- **SOUTHERN MOORS**
- **NORTHERN MOORS**

Circular Walks - South Pennines
- **BRONTE COUNTRY**
- **ILKLEY MOOR**
- **CALDERDALE**
- **SOUTHERN PENNINES**

Circular Walks - Lancashire
- **BOWLAND**
- **PENDLE & THE RIBBLE**
- **WEST PENNINE MOORS**

Circular Walks - North Pennines
- **TEESDALE**
- **EDEN VALLEY**

Yorkshire Pub Walks
- **HARROGATE/WHARFE VALLEY**
- **HAWORTH/AIRE VALLEY**

- **YORKSHIRE DALES CYCLE WAY**
- **WEST YORKSHIRE CYCLE WAY**
- **MOUNTAIN BIKING - WEST & SOUTH YORKSHIRE**
- **AIRE VALLEY BIKING GUIDE**
- **CALDERDALE BIKING GUIDE**
- **GLASGOW Clyde Valley & Loch Lomond (Biking)**

- **YORK WALKS** *City Theme Walks*

Send for a detailed current catalogue and pricelist

BRONTË COUNTRY

Paul Hannon

HILLSIDE

HILLSIDE
PUBLICATIONS
12 Broadlands
Shann Park
Keighley
West Yorkshire
BD20 6HX

First published 1987
This fully revised and extended 4th edition
first published 2002

ISBN 1 870141 69 5

*Cover illustrations: 'Wuthering Heights' - around Top Withins
Back: Worth Valley; Wainman's Pinnacle, Earl Crag; Wycoller
(Paul Hannon Picture Library)*

*Page 1: Milestone, Thornton-in-Craven;
Hill Top, Penistone Hill, Haworth
Page 3: Packhorse bridge, Wycoller*

Printed in Great Britain by
Carnmor Print
95-97 London Road
Preston
Lancashire
PR1 4BA

CONTENTS

INTRODUCTION

The extensive region of hill country between the Yorkshire Dales and the Peak District is the richly varied Heritage Area known as the South Pennines. The part of it covered within these pages is its northernmost tract, lying between Skipton and Calderdale. The Aire Valley forms a well defined eastern boundary, while the West Craven corridor between Skipton and Colne fulfils a similar role to the west. Southwards, the Pennine moors form a lofty boundary with Calderdale.

Though not the area's geographical centre, Haworth is certainly the focal point. It was made internationally famous by the Brontë sisters, who themselves played a part in promoting the neighbouring moorland. Haworth looks over the Worth Valley, which aided by its steam railway, drives a wedge into the heart of the high moors which dominate this broader southern half of the area. Reservoirs and gritstone outcrops occur with regularity hereabouts, but tend to fade away as the Pennines progress northwards to South Craven and West Craven. Here is an area of pocket moorlands parcelled between rolling valley sides and independent villages. Lothersdale, Cowling, Foulridge and Cononley typify these settlements, which today act largely as dormitories for towns such as Keighley, Skipton and Colne. Most are, or until recently were, dominated by 'dark satanic mills', a reminder that this is the fringe of the industrial West Riding and East Lancashire. Sadly most of these village centrepieces have either been abandoned, converted, or even dismantled in recent years.

Within the area the more traditional industry of quarrying (almost exclusively gritstone, but with a rare showing of limestone) was once quite extensive, though rarely on any large scale. Lead mining also made a contribution in one location. Farming, as always, labours on through everything thrown at it, for in this harsh landscape little else but sheep farming is practicable: a timely reminder that the last thing a hill farmer needs is gates left open, or walkers' dogs running loose. The grand old man of long distance walks, the Pennine Way, runs through the area from Top Withins to Thornton-in-Craven, and several of the routes share a mile or two of its celebrated course. Additionally, lesser known, less demanding routes such as the Pendle Way, Brontë Way and Trans-Pennine Way are also encountered.

Though of modest proportions this area embraces no less than three 'counties', the walks being split between West Yorkshire, North Yorkshire and Lancashire. Despite what modern maps may claim, the Barnoldswick area is true Yorkshire, a corner of God's Own Country

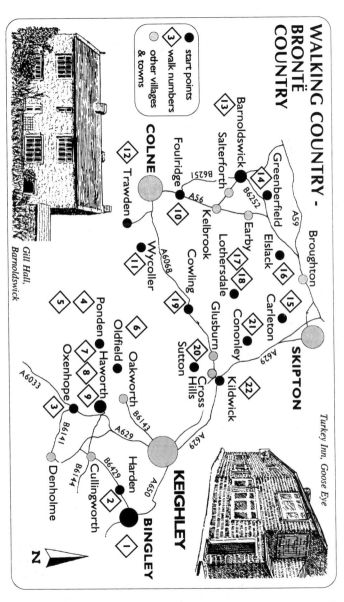

WALKING COUNTRY -
BRONTË
COUNTRY

● start points
③ walk numbers
○ other villages & towns

Gill Hall, Barnoldswick

Turkey Inn, Goose Eye

BRONTË
COUNTRY

Barnoldswick ⑬
Salterforth
Greenberfield
Foulridge ⑭
COLNE
⑫ Trawden
Kelbrook
Earby ⑰⑱
Elslack
Broughton
Lothersdale
Wycoller ⑪
Cowling
⑩
A6068
Glusburn ⑲
Cononley ㉑
Carleton ⑮
⑯
SKIPTON
⑤
④
Ponden
Oldfield
⑥
Haworth ⑦⑧⑨
Oxenhope ③
Denholme
Cullingworth ②
Harden
Oakworth
Sutton
Cross Hills ⑳
Kildwick ㉒
KEIGHLEY
BINGLEY
①
N

that since 1974 has been mischievously purloined by the Red Rose. In truth, several walks cross county boundaries, an indication that on the ground, at least, such political nonsense is largely immaterial: the drystone walls and the views differ little!

So what will this collection of walks reveal? Well, most of the area's finest landmarks, including Earl Crag, Pinhaw Beacon, Weets Hill and Boulsworth Hill, and such Worth Valley favourites as Haworth Moor, Top Withins and Nab Hill. The rivers Aire and Worth are followed, as is the towpath of the Leeds-Liverpool Canal. Little valleys are secreted all over the region, some of the finest being Wycoller Dean, Goit Stock, Sutton Clough and Newsholme Dean. Without doubt, the Brontë Country caters for all.

Getting around

The area is ideally placed for walkers from the surrounding towns of West Yorkshire and East Lancashire, and is becoming increasingly popular as a holiday destination. Its advantage over many areas is that there are always ample nearby distractions when poor weather intervenes. Almost all the starting points are accessible by bus, some also by train.

Using the guide

Each walk is self-contained, with essential information being followed by a simple map and a concise route description. Dovetailed in between are notes of features along the way, and interspersed are illustrations which capture the flavour of the walks and record many items of interest. Essential route description has been highlighted in bold, in order to make it easily accessible in amongst the other snippets of information. The sketch maps serve only to identify the location of the routes rather than the fine detail, and whilst the description should be sufficient to guide you around, an Ordnance Survey map is strongly recommended.

To gain the most from a walk, the detail of the 1:25,000 scale maps is unsurpassed. They also serve to vary walks as desired, giving an improved picture of one's surroundings and the availability of linking paths. Just two maps cover the walks in this book (almost all being found on the former):

- Outdoor Leisure 21 - *South Pennines*
- Explorer 288 - *Bradford & Huddersfield*

Also useful for general planning are two Landranger maps at the scale of 1:50,000: *103, Blackburn & Burnley*; and *104, Leeds, Bradford & Harrogate*.

HAWORTH

Haworth ceased to be just another village in the 19th century when the fame of the Brontës spread, though it took until relatively recently to become a full blown tourist honeypot. Focal point is the main street, lined with shops and cafes unashamedly aimed at visitors, many of whom are not quite sure why they're here: some view the Brontë connection not unlike the 'Summer Wine' celebrity status of not so distant Holmfirth! Despite a by-pass the poor old main street still resounds to the bustle of cars nudging gawping pedestrians from its setts into the gutters. The street climbs steeply to the parish church of St. Michael, suitably surrounded by pubs. Only its tower would be recognisable to the Brontës, the rest having been rebuilt around 1880. Inside, the Brontë Vault holds the remains of all but Anne, whose grave can be found overlooking the sea at Scarborough. It is said some 40,000 villagers are at rest in Haworth churchyard.

Behind the church is the parsonage, an elegant Georgian building of 1779. Just across the cobbled side street is the old school, where two of the sisters and Branwell taught. The parsonage is now a museum of its former occupants, very much the spiritual heart of the Brontë scene. A comprehensive Brontë-themed shop is attached. Only minutes away is the open moorland that so inspired the sisters, while back down the main street is Haworth's second major attraction, the preserved steam railway. Although Haworth is at neither terminus, its station, with its goods yard, is at the hub of things. The railway actually leaves the Worth Valley near Oakworth to follow Bridgehouse Beck past Haworth to Oxenhope, a reminder of its original purpose, to serve the mills. Haworth has its own youth hostel, half a mile from the rail station off the Keighley road.

The Black Bull,
Haworth

THE BRONTËS

Patrick Brunty was born in 1777, eldest of 10 children raised in conditions of some hardship in County Down. Through a fortunate acquaintance he had the opportunity to study at Cambridge, and he amended his name in recognition of his hero Lord Nelson (who had become Duke of Brontë). After a spell in southern England he came north to Yorkshire, initially to Dewsbury. He began his curacy at Hartshead in 1811, and lodged at a nearby farm. The following year he married Maria Branwell, a Cornishwoman, and they took up residence at Clough House, Hightown. Here their first two children, Maria and Elizabeth, were born.

In 1815 Brontë moved to Thornton, though the Bell Chapel is now merely a few remains in the shadow of the later church. In a small house in the village street the remaining four children were born, Charlotte in 1816, Patrick Branwell in 1817, Emily Jane in 1818, and Anne in 1820. No sooner was the family complete then it was on the move again, this time to their celebrated home, the parsonage at Haworth. Here all but one of them were to end their lives, indeed the children lost their mother the very next year. The death of the elder daughters in 1825 left the four other children to attain adulthood.

The three sisters departed on numerous occasions to spend largely unsuccessful spells as teachers and governesses in other parts of the region, while Branwell, the only brother, showed promise as an artist. His progress, however, soon faltered, and after a spell as a railway clerk at Luddenden Foot, in the Calder Valley, he returned home: stricken by illness he saw out his closing years as a regular of the Black Bull, adjacent to the church. Meanwhile the sisters had also returned to the fold, but in their cases to begin their pitifully short literary careers. In an age when such activity by women was frowned upon, the sisters' first works appeared under the pseudonyms Currer, Ellis and Acton Bell, with each retaining their initials.

When the first novels were published Emily and Anne had little time to enjoy any acclaim, for their deaths rapidly followed the demise of Branwell in 1848. Anne was buried in Scarborough, where the sea air had offered no escape from the common killer tuberculosis, then known as consumption, that accounted for all but Charlotte. Charlotte's first published novel *Jane Eyre* was followed by further works, during which time she enjoyed critical acclaim and popularity. She even survived long enough to marry her father's curate, the Rev.

Arthur Bell Nicholls in 1854, though tragically her flame was also to burn out the very next year, still not 39. Thus Patrick Brontë was to outlive all his children, attaining the ripe old age of 84.

What makes the story of the Brontë sisters so memorable is the nature of the background to their literary achievements, notably the adversity the family had faced, and more appreciably still the brooding mass of moorland beyond their Haworth home, where they sought and found untold inspiration. Listed is a chronology of the novels' publication.

1847
Jane Eyre (Charlotte)
Wuthering Heights (Emily)
Agnes Grey (Anne)
1848
The Tenant of Wildfell Hall (Anne)
1849
Shirley (Charlotte)
1853
Villette (Charlotte)
1857
The Professor (Charlotte)

Haworth Parsonage

1

DRUID'S ALTAR & ST. IVES

START *Bingley*   *Grid ref. SE 106394*

DISTANCE *6¼ miles*

ORDNANCE SURVEY MAPS
1:50,000
Landranger 104 - Leeds, Bradford & Harrogate
1:25,000
Explorer 288 - Bradford & Huddersfield

ACCESS *Start from the parish church on the main road, near Ireland Bridge over the Aire. Town centre car parks. Served by bus and train from Keighley, Bradford and Leeds. An alternative start (by car) is St. Ives, whose car park is reached off the Harden Road (B6429).*

Amid richly wooded surroundings, the charismatic viewpoint of the Druid's Altar complements the fascinating St. Ives estate.

S Bingley is a bustling industrial town which has happily retained some of its older corners, notably the environs of the parish church. In the spacious park is the Georgian Town Hall (formerly the Ferrand family's Myrtle Grove); while nearby is the Market Hall, quite recently restored to its rightful place. A remarkable aspect of the town is that the river Aire flowing parallel to its busy main street has repelled any development on its western bank. Indeed, I have seen a kingfisher within a five minute walk of the overloaded main street.

From the cobbled Old Main Street by the parish church, take the B6429 Bingley-Harden road over Ireland Bridge on the river Aire. The bridge links the historic *Old White Horse Inn* with the *Brown Cow Inn*, dispensing the prize-winning ales of Timothy Taylors of Keighley. **Turn sharp right along Ireland Street, quickly turning right again in front of a factory. An unsurfaced road then heads upstream in tandem with the river, through increasingly wooded**

surrounds. **This access road later leaves the river to run beneath wooded slopes to Raven Royd.** This lovely old house features arch-headed mullioned windows, and it fronts a characterful farmyard scene. **Pass to its right, on through the yard, and straight on the continuing walled access track to Cophurst.**

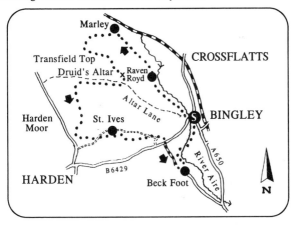

Pass left of the house and out into a field. A cart track continues on beneath a wooded bank, and behind the grassy knoll of Hutler Hill to a track junction. Advance to a gate in front, and a grassy track runs on to a stile onto an access road from the scattered hamlet of Marley. Just over to the right is another fine old building, that of Marley Hall. **Go left the few yards towards Blakey Cottage with its 1694 datestone above the door. Turn up its near side on a steep, stone paved road, and approaching the house above, bear right on a branch to a gate. A solid track slants up the increasingly colourful pasture towards the lone house at Transfield Hole.** All of this grand section enjoys extensive views over the Aire Valley. While the Rombalds Moor skyline might be fairly timeless, the lower ground is dominated by recent additions such as dual carriageway, housing development and golf course.

A **rougher continuation track continues above the house, slanting up Marley Brow to eventually peter out. Rise to a stile just above, and a good path climbs a bracken-choked enclosure. When it forks bear right up towards the top corner.** Just short of the corner a thinner, sunken pathway bears left, merging with a higher path to run along the top of this moorland enclosure. With a wall just above, the path runs delightfully through the heather terrain of Transfield Top, ultimately to emerge via a stile onto an access road. Cross straight over and along the few yards to the Druid's Altar. Here sizeable gritstone outcrops form a well defined edge in colourful open country, the finest location from which to survey the aforementioned view. If the Druids did offer sacrifices here (!), they certainly chose a grand spot.

At the end of the rocks leave the edge on a path running the short distance 'inland' to meet Altar Lane. This old road now serves as a good walkers'/bikers' route from Bingley directly up to the Druid's Altar. It continues outside the St. Ives estate wall to end at the crest of the Keighley-Harden road. Straight across, a stile/gateway give access to the St. Ives estate.

The country estate of St. Ives was at one time owned by the Knights Templar and Knights Hospitallers, and later by the monks of Rievaulx Abbey. The estate passed to the influential Ferrand family in 1636, and finally into public ownership in 1928. Around 400 acres cover much of this hillside between Harden and Bingley. Within its high walls are a superb mix of woodland, moorland and farmland, along with a golf course and a sports turf research centre. It was only in the 1990s that the fine choice of paths became recorded as a labyrinthine public rights of way network. The 19th century mansion was renovated to provide a nursing home, with some of the redundant Home Farm buildings planned as a specialised riding centre.

At once leave the main bridleway by turning right through a stile onto a good path. This soon enters a belt of trees, remaining near the boundary wall until confronted by a lesser wall. Here the path turns left to begin a long, steady descent by the upper part of the golf course and aptly-named Heather Park to Lady Blantyre's Rock. En route, a branch path through scattered woodland visits the Ferrand Monument, a popular landmark at which to linger. Lady Blantyre's Rock is a large gritstone boulder where the eponymous woman often came to sojourn. After her death in 1875, her son-in-law William Ferrand placed an inscribed tablet here. Being something of a dignitary himself, the adjacent noble obelisk was erected after his death in 1889.

Below Lady Blantyre's Rock the broad path delves into deeper woodland before swinging left, with the main path soon running alongside the sizeable Coppice Pond. Below this the road through the estate is crossed to another path which runs below the mansion itself. **Again ignore branches to the right to meet the estate road again. Either remain on it, or take a path sharp right to drop to a path along the bottom edge of the wood. Go left along this to rejoin the road at a lodge.** Follow this briefly right, but as it winds down towards the B6429 Harden-Bingley road, **bear left on a broad path back into trees. This quickly forks: take the right branch, which descends to a gap-stile onto the road.**

Cross the often busy road with care and escape with relief down peaceful Beckfoot Lane. At the bottom it loses its surface as it runs past a converted mill to reach Beck Foot. This is an idyllic location, with an 18th century arched bridge, a ford and some desirable cottages. **Don't cross the tempting bridge, but take a stile on the left and head on through the field.** With the river Aire just below, and Myrtle Park opposite, this complete greenery makes it impossible to believe we are on the very edge of a town the size of Bingley. **Rising to pass a solitary house and into the trees, the path runs on and descends to a large open space before crossing the Aire by a substantial iron bridge.** Built to commemorate the Festival of Britain in 1951, it gives access to Myrtle Park.

For the town centre go straight up through the park. **For Ireland Bridge turn left on the riverside walk to conclude.** This pleasant little stroll clings to the river, and en route passes a picnic site, steps up onto Market Street, and the Ailsa Well. This latter feature is identified by a sign on a wall by a tasteful memorial: just through a gap in the wall and across a track, a flight of stone steps descends to a stone trough with water tinkling in, all hidden in greenery.

Lady Blantyre's Rock, St. Ives

William Ferrand Monument, St Ives

15

2

GOIT STOCK WOOD & HARDEN MOOR

START *Harden*   *Grid ref. SE 085383*

DISTANCE *5½ miles*

ORDNANCE SURVEY MAPS
1:50,000
Landranger 104 - Leeds, Bradford & Harrogate
1:25,000
Outdoor Leisure 21 - South Pennines
Explorer 288 - Bradford & Huddersfield

ACCESS *Start from the village centre. Roadside parking, ideally on the Wilsden road. Served by bus from Bingley and Keighley.*

A brilliantly colourful walk, with a memorable contrast of woodland and open moor.

S Harden is a sizeable village with strong links with Bingley, where its beck joins the Aire. Its once dominant mills are now being replaced by housing. The *Golden Fleece* pub is centrally placed on the main road. **From the staggered crossroads turn along the Wilsden road to descend to Harden Beck.** Across the bridge stands the *Malt Shovel*, a popular pub with a long history and a fine floral display.

The Malt Shovel, Harden Beck

Without crossing, turn right along the unsurfaced Goit Stock Lane. Beyond some housing this runs pleasantly alongside Harden Beck through largely wooded surrounds. At a cattle-grid note the little falls on a bend above a former mill, with a branch emerging into the beck through a well built stone arch. **On reaching a caravan park, keep straight on the road to the far end. Passing a cottage, a broad path goes straight ahead into woodland, with the beck having returned to present its finest section.**

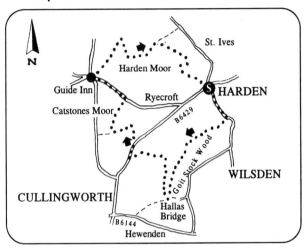

This lovely walk marches upstream through the trees of Goit Stock Wood. This is a hugely attractive section decorated by springtime bluebells: an early delight is the confluence of Cow House Beck beneath a craggy knoll. **Gradually steeper slopes close in to reach Goit Stock Falls.** This is a beautiful drop over a craggy wall into a deep bowl, the centrepiece of these glorious woodlands. **A handrail assists in surmounting the little cliff before the delightful amble resumes past a smaller waterfall to reach a broad track at Hallas Bridge. Cross the bridge and leave the track at once, on a short path up to a stile on the right. A small field is crossed to re-enter woods on a level path. Leaving by a stile at the far end, a large field surrounded on three sides by woodland leads down to a footbridge on Cow House Beck. Up the slope behind, turn sharp left to shadow a wall along the top of the large pasture above the beck. Part way on,**

a stile sends the path over the wall, only to return at another before the end of the field. The wall is now shadowed by a decent path above the beck, all the way to the B6429 Cullingworth-Harden road. This is another enjoyable section above colourful slopes, with Cullingworth church spire prominent. The road is joined alongside a bus stop, convenient if you can't go another step!

Cross to the footway and go right a short distance, then left up the delightful course of Dolphin Lane. Engulfed in undergrowth, this slender bridlepath bizarrely merits a standard roadsign! **Part sunken in its upper half, it rises onto the moorland base of Catstones Hill. Follow a good path left until almost at the corner gate off the moor, then double back right.** Cullingworth is outspread to the left, with Black Moor behind it and Ovenden Moor windfarm on the long skyline high above. **Before the corner a thin path effects a modest short-cut by slanting up from a stile in the adjacent fence, meeting the public footpath that has come up from the very corner. Quickly broadening, it winds up through an old quarry site largely reclaimed by nature.**

The path ascends through long defunct quarries before rising more gently across the moor. After levelling out, with modern quarry workings close by ahead, the path passes through a discernible section of Catstones Ring, an ancient trench in a grassy break in the heather. **Emerging onto a road, go left for a short half-mile to the *Guide Inn*.** This local landmark features a fine pictorial south-facing wall, and appropriately presides over a hilltop junction of ways.

The Guide Inn

Ignoring the roads, turn right on a broad rough road along the edge of Harden Moor, it narrows to a bridlepath part way along. Views ahead feature a Rombalds Moor skyline, including Baildon Hill; a couple of boundary stones inscribed 'P' are passed along the base of the wall. **At a T-junction at the end, take a kissing-gate in the fence on the right and follow a superb, partly flagged old way striking across the open moor.** The heather upland of Harden Moor is an open access area maintained by the local authority, and is popular with all manner of leisure user.

At a crossroads turn left to a gritstone outcrop, then down to a wall corner. Remain on this wallside bridle-track to the head of Deep Cliff Hole. At the path's lowest point - marked by a stile in the wall - fork right on a thinner, level path. This runs between the moor and the steep wooded drop of the clough. This is a super section through a colourful mix of birch woodland, scrub, bracken and small boulders. **Avoiding any lesser forks it runs on to approach a wall, bearing right to reach the wall corner at a few small outcrops. The path now drops down to leave the trees at a stile.**

Slant down a small field to a hidden stile onto an access road. Turn right on this, in around the wooded environs of the stream. As it turns to climb steeply away, take a gate/stile on the left where a grassy path crosses a field to the house at Spring Farm. The path neatly skirts the garden and resumes to Spring House, just ahead. Immediately before it take a narrow, enclosed footpath down to the left. This quickly accompanies the beck downstream, passing modern housing on the site of a mill. Advance straight on to join the main road in the village centre, rather handily alongside the pub.

Goit Stock Falls

3

NAB HILL

START Oxenhope   Grid ref. SE 031352

DISTANCE 6½ miles

ORDNANCE SURVEY MAPS
1:50,000
Landranger 104 - Leeds, Bradford & Harrogate
1:25,000
Outdoor Leisure 21 - South Pennines

ACCESS Start from Mill Lane outside the railway station car park. Parking on nearby Cross Lane. As well as trains from Keighley via Haworth, Oxenhope is also served by bus from Keighley.

A string of old ways explore the moorland slopes above Oxenhope, giving splendid views.

S Oxenhope is a fine example of a Pennine mill community. The village sits in a basin with steep hills rising on almost all sides, through pastures to the layers of moor above. While its illustrious neighbour Haworth draws the tourists, Oxenhope takes a back seat and seems quite happy to stay largely unaltered. Recent changes, however, have seen old mills torn down to be replaced by modern housing. The squat church looks down from its lofty perch, witnessing, among other things, a now-famous annual event, the straw race. This colourful pub crawl is also a great charity fund-raiser, incorporating the village centre *Bay Horse* among its more distantly ranged ports of call.

From the station entrance turn left along Mill Lane, quickly becoming Harry Lane which climbs steeply to the A6033 Keighley-Hebden Bridge road. Cross and resume up the narrow and steep Dark Lane. At the first opportunity go right along a quiet back road (Yate Lane) to emerge by the Post office in Lowertown. Go left a short way up Denholme Road, then bear right on Jew Lane. Avoid further, lesser forks right until the handful of houses at Back

Leeming, where bear right on a level cul-de-sac road. Becoming a rougher access road it crosses a bridge to Egypt House. From a stile just above it, an enclosed path climbs to a farm road at the corner of Leeming Reservoir. Across the embankment of the 1877 dam is Leeming, a small settlement dominated by its former mill, and with a pub, the *Lamb Inn*.

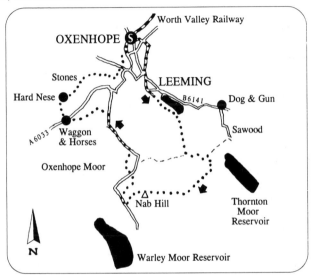

Ignoring the embankment road, cross straight over on another farm road to a fork, where go left across another field. As the farm road climbs away, advance straight on a fieldpath above the reservoir. Dropping to a footbridge near the reservoir head, the cairn on Nab Hill is seen seemingly very high above. From the bridge a part embanked path climbs the bank behind to a stile onto the moor. The path then rises to a long-superfluous stone stile before crossing the beck on the left at a concrete ford. Rise up above the stream to reach a water conduit, which can be crossed by a stile on the right-hand of two bridges. Head up the slope again to the prominent trees above to join the clear track of Sawood Lane.

Turn left on this, soon winding up to a wall, with a track junction a few yards to the left. Turn right through the gate to begin the ascent of part sunken Hambleton Lane between old walls. Half

21

way up, escape by a gate on the right, from where a sunken way slants across the moor to the grassy spoilheaps of old quarries. The cairn on Nab Hill beckons further along the moor edge as the grand path runs between these knolls and abandoned stones. The tall, flailing turbines of Ovenden Moor windfarm form an eerie sight looming large just across the flat moortop, but more impressive are the massive views over Leeming, Oxenhope and much further beyond.

Beyond the quarry site the path curves around the heads of Little Clough and Great Clough, which are divided by a moorland edge and a few more quarry remains. Just above the second clough some abandoned slates remain stacked, as if awaiting imminent removal. It is then a short stroll to the waiting cairn on Nab Hill. Set amid further small-scale remains at an altitude of 1475ft/450m, the cairn is a fine specimen with a curved arm incorporating a shelter for the solitary rambler. Locally just 'the Nab', this is a place to linger and savour the extensive view. Westwards are the Lancashire heights of Boulsworth Hill and Pendle Hill; northwards beyond Brontë Country is a magnificent panorama of Dales peaks, including Ingleborough, Penyghent, Fountains Fell, Buckden Pike and Great Whernside.

From a more capacious stone shelter on the knoll just below, a thin path runs on past a pile of stones to a cairn with extended triangular arms on marginally higher ground. The path then curves around the slope to drop down to the broader quarry path across to the left. At the same time, Fly Flatts Reservoir (Warley Moor Reservoir on maps) appears ahead. This high-altitude sheet of water is home to a sailing club. The path curves down beneath old spoilheaps to a stile onto Nab Water Lane. This climbs to run past the windfarm to the isolated *Withens Hotel* before dropping towards Halifax.

Turn down this for a mere hundred yards, and head off through a gateway on the right. A faint path contours across the slope to a wall corner. Advance along the crumbled walltop, noting that every wall in view, including many across to Oxenhope Moor on the left, is equally redundant. At the third descending wall drop down to a stile on a water conduit, and thence down to rejoin the road. A continuing path sets straight off across the moor opposite from an old stile with a benchmark on the stone post. Alternatively, simply remain on the moorland road to the prominent mast ahead. The path, meanwhile, rises with an old wall to largely fade at a wall corner. Advance a little to the stone-walled conduit, which is followed right on a good grassy track. At the stone bridge carrying Far Peat Lane over it, rejoin the adjacent road.

Just beyond the bend under the prominent mast, as a steep descent is about to commence, take a stile on the left. Two field tops are crossed to join the rough Intake Lane. Rise left on this, briefly, before dropping to the *Waggon & Horses* pub on the A6033 Hebden Bridge road. Sadly in late 2001 this had ceased trading. **Cross straight over and down a rough access road, going right at the bottom past Hard Nese farm and along to emerge onto the patch of moorland known as Stones.** This is a locally popular heathery island directly above Oxenhope, surrounded by green pastures. **As the track goes sharp left, take the path rising to a wall corner to run pleasantly along the crest.**

At the end the path meets a track by a house: go straight over and along a footpath past a smashing house, Olde Croft, boasting mullioned windows and a lovely garden. The path runs out into a drive, and as its swings right a flagged path goes straight on at a path crossroads: here take one to the left, through a gap-stile and down through a tiny gate to lead down a fieldside. The parish church is just across to the right. **A little gate in the bottom corner sends an enclosed snicket down onto Shaw Lane on the edge of the village. Turn right to the junction with the main road, then take a surfaced path on the left. This descends through the park to swing around to emerge onto Cross Lane. Turn down this to Mill Lane to finish.**

St. Mary the Virgin, Oxenhope

4

TOP WITHINS &
PONDEN CLOUGH

START *Ponden*   *Grid ref. SD 995370*

DISTANCE *5 miles*

ORDNANCE SURVEY MAPS
1:50,000
Landranger 103 - Blackburn & Burnley
1:25,000
Outdoor Leisure 21 - South Pennines

ACCESS *Start from the dam of Ponden Reservoir, west of Stanbury at Scar Top. Reached by the cul-de-sac Ponden Lane from Ponden Mill on the road below the dam. Car parking on the road on the south side of the reservoir. Stanbury is served by bus from Keighley via Haworth.*

A visit to two outstanding landmarks, one natural, one literary, on the moors south of the Worth Valley.

S **Head west on the road along the south shore of the reservoir.** Directly ahead is Ponden Clough, with its lower reaches well wooded, a riot of colour culminating abruptly where two tumbling rocky becks merge. **At the end of the reservoir the road climbs to Ponden Hall.** Ponden Hall is a characterful structure perched high above the reservoir. For centuries it was the home of the Heaton family, and Emily Brontë was a regular visitor. She portrayed the house as Thrushcross Grange, the Linton home in *Wuthering Heights*. An inscription above the door informs that the original house of 1634 was rebuilt in 1807.

   A rough road climbs away from the hall. Keep straight on to the brow, then bear left up the walled farm road to Height Laithe. Ignoring the turning to the farm, head straight up the walled track

onto the foot of the open moor. **Advance straight on the wallside track, and beyond the wall corner keep on a little further to a waymark. Here take the path rising left to a crumbling wall above the barn at Upper Ponden. At another waymark turn right up the nearside of the wall, a good path rising to a brow, amid increasing heather.** Ponden Clough is revealed below and Ponden Reservoir re-appears further back, while the view north features an unbroken moorland skyline around past the Wolf Stones.

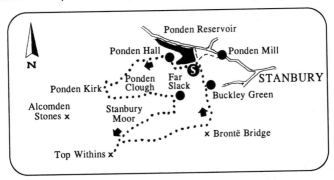

As the wall parts company, **the clear path continues on across the moor, a smashing stride as it runs more closely above the edge of the steeper drop.** The improving prospect of the clough shows the southerly feeder of Middle Moor Clough to good effect, while the Alcomden Stones occupy the skyline directly ahead. **Crossing the slabbed floor of the northerly feeder, the path doubles back out to reach Ponden Kirk, in view ahead.**

Ponden Kirk is the Peniston Crag of *Wuthering Heights*. It requires little imagination to visualise this backdrop to Cathy's and Heathcliff's tormented story: beneath the crag is the natural aperture to which Cathy makes reference. Legend has it that should a young maid undertake the crawl through this dark, grimy orifice beneath the crag, then she shall be married within the year. Just up behind is an old sheepfold, and a curious sign advising the grid reference of this lonely spot. The prepondrance of guideposts does take the edge off being on the moors, and both principal features of the walk suffer the same fate. As regards the Japanese 'wording' that frequents them, well my countless excursions to Ponden have never yet witnessed an Oriental visitor!

The path continues round to the southern feeder stream at Middle Moor Clough, doubling back a little to a junction just above the stream. Ignoring the steep path down into the clough, cross this smaller stream and resume on the path rising gently away, now above the southern rim. This is another grand stride, the path improving on a gentle decline to meet a wall. On the skyline just above are the modest cluster of the Master Stones. The path follows the wall steadily down to a fence-stile above the house at Far Slack. If omitting Top Withins cross it and follow the access road to pick up the route at Buckley Green, near the end of the walk.

For the full route, don't cross the stile but turn up the path, climbing by fence then wall past the steeper slopes of the Master Stones to meet the broad track of the Pennine Way. Turn right on this for a pleasant march across Stanbury Moor. Emerging from a broad groove in the heather, Top Withins soon appears ahead. A steady rise, much on stone flags, leads quickly to a path junction signed for Haworth at a double ruin: the return path turns down this. Two minutes further up the path are the more famous ruins of Top Withins.

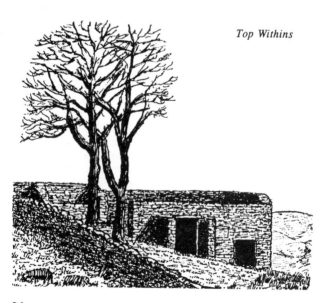

Top Withins

TOP WITHENS.
THIS FARMHOUSE HAS BEEN ASSOCIATED WITH "WUTHERING HEIGHTS," THE EARNSHAW HOME IN EMILY BRONTË'S NOVEL.
THE BUILDINGS, EVEN WHEN COMPLETE, BORE NO RESEMBLANCE TO THE HOUSE SHE DESCRIBED,
BUT THE SITUATION MAY HAVE BEEN IN HER MIND WHEN SHE WROTE OF THE MOORLAND SETTING OF THE HEIGHTS.
THIS PLAQUE HAS BEEN PLACED HERE IN RESPONSE TO MANY INQUIRIES.
BRONTË SOCIETY 1964

At Top Withins

Top Withins, or simply 'Withins' (as Withins and Lower Withins are now only piles of stones), is a famous ruin where one requires solitude in order to imbibe the atmosphere. A Pennine Way information board, a small bothy in a dingy outhouse, and an array of outdoor seating all contribute to the demise of any 'wild' feeling. Top Withins is regarded as the Earnshaw home in Emily's classic *Wuthering Heights*. It is difficult to imagine that this lonely outpost was once a home, but whether or not Emily Brontë actually visualised Heathcliff here, one can readily imagine her story being enacted in this bleak and inhospitable moorland setting which is, indeed 'wuthering'.

Retrace steps for a minute or so then branch right, a well-worn path descending to cross the infant South Dean Beck. This popular path (the main route to Top Withins) runs on above the forming clough, encountering a number of stiles as it enters old pastures to arrive above the rubble that was once the farm of Virginia, itself high above the Brontë Bridge. Keep straight on, treading a part causeyed path to a ladder-stile into a green pasture. Head away briefly with the crumbling wall, then bear left on a faint path to another ladder-stile. This re-admits onto moorland, and a fine green path runs on across two Landrover tracks to a stile between enclosing walls. At the second track we are rejoined by the Pennine Way.

A splendid green path runs on between walls to rapidly reach a fine edge overlooking the Ponden scene. This impressive prospect centres on Ponden Reservoir directly below, with farms and fields rising to Keighley Moor opposite. Over to the left is Ponden Clough. **Descend the wallside path to a rough road, going briefly right by the house at Buckley Green then sharp left on the short-lived drive down to the houses at Buckley House.** At Buckley Green lived Timmy Feather, who died in 1910 and is remembered as the last handloom weaver. **Just in front, take a stile on the right and descend a pleasant enclosed way, swinging left at the bottom as a rough lane to emerge past the farm at Rush Isles and conclude at the reservoir corner.**

27

5

WATERSHEDDLES

START Ponden   Grid ref. SD 995370

DISTANCE 6 miles

ORDNANCE SURVEY MAPS
1:50,000
Landranger 103 - Blackburn & Burnley
1:25,000
Outdoor Leisure 21 - South Pennines

ACCESS Start from the road on the south side of Ponden Reservoir, west of Stanbury at Scar Top. Reached by the cul-de-sac Ponden Lane from Ponden Mill on the road just below the dam. Stanbury is served by bus from Keighley via Haworth.

Wild country on the Lancashire border, featuring the infant river Worth and some rough but characterful moorland above it. The outward half of this walk traces the route of the Brontë Way.

⑤ **Head west on the road along the south shore of the reservoir.** Directly ahead is Ponden Clough, with its lower reaches well wooded, a riot of colour culminating abruptly where two tumbling rocky becks merge. **At the end of the reservoir the road climbs to Ponden Hall.** This characterful structure perches high above the reservoir. Emily Brontë visited the Heaton family here and portrayed the house as Thrushcross Grange, the Linton home in *Wuthering Heights*. An inscription above the door informs that the original house of 1634 was rebuilt in 1807.

A rough road climbs away from the hall. Keep straight on over the brow to descend to the rear of an enviably sited house. Down below is the slender upper arm of the reservoir. **A green path runs on between fences above the house to a bend. As the Pennine Way turns sharp right down this green way, our way takes the stile in front and along a similar way. At Whitestone Farm a diversion goes left a few**

yards to a ladder-stile, then past the garden and on to regain its original course at the far end. Just a little further turn up a few yards to a gateway on the right, and slant down the field to the far corner.

A simple bridge on Whitestone Clough precedes a wallside climb to Old Snap. Keep left of the farmhouse and on a short grassy way to a brow, with the upper reaches of the Worth Valley below. From this point the Way follows a concession path to the Pennine watershed. Go left on the inviting green path along the bank top and crumbling wallside. At the end a stile admits to a green walled way, leading to a ladder-stile at the far end. Across the now narrow valley is the impressive facade of Moor Lodge, a Victorian shooting lodge currently operating as a fashionable pine retailer. High on the skyline behind are the Wolf Stones.

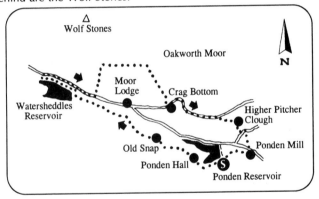

Marker posts guide the initially faint path down to enter the deeper confines of the infant river Worth, merely a small stream. A path then runs upstream. The bizarre surround of rhododendrons is a hangover from the heyday of Moor Lodge, nevertheless this is a very colourful quarter with bracken, scrub and a few rocks overlooking the stream. Although one or two moist moments feature, this really is a grand section. The confines narrow to reach a footbridge on the Worth. The Worth runs a 10 mile course from Watersheddles to enter the river Aire beyond Keighley, and the little patch of grassy bank makes a good spot to halt awhile.

Resume upstream, the path encountering several stiles before rising steadily up the bank. The path runs at mid height through a couple of old walls, and with the grassy dam of Watersheddles

Reservoir appearing just ahead, a large boundary stone is reached. This was erected in 1985 to mark the departure of the Brontë Way from God's Own Country into Lancashire.

Boundary stone, Watersheddles

From the ladder-stile beyond, the path slants up to a barn and on to a Brontë Way information board by the embankment. **Over a ladder-stile a good path runs on through a strip of heather alongside the water, parallel with the moorland road to Laneshaw Bridge.** The crossing of the stile brings Lancashire's most famous natural landmark into view, as Pendle Hill appears through the gap beyond the head of the reservoir. The Wolf Stones break the moorland skyline much closer to hand up to the right. Watersheddles is an apt name for this Pennine watershed reservoir, which suffers a curious identity crisis. Though it is within Yorkshire's gathering grounds and belongs to Yorkshire Water, the errant wanderings of the county boundary mean it is actually located entirely within Lancashire.

At the end another stile exits the reservoir wall, and here forsake the Brontë Way by joining the adjacent road. Double back on this outside the full length of the reservoir wall, and along to the county boundary. It is a sad reflection of the times that neither Yorkshire nor Lancashire are mentioned, merely Bradford and Pendle - hardly the same is it? On the right side stands a Keighley/Trawden boundary stone. Also on the boundary is the Hanging Stone, otherwise Watersheddles Cross, visible on the moor above. **Within a further 200 yards, take a ladder-stile on the left and ascend the reedy pasture. This is an escape from the reedy walled way alongside. Towards the top take a small gate onto the head of this way, and another just above onto open moorland.**

Advance directly away onto the moor, tracing a distinct grassy pathway through the heather, shadowed by a line of basic shooting shelters. Just before these end the path does likewise. Happily it is time to turn sharp right, thus evading the uninviting terrain and crossing towards a wall corner visible further east. Maintain a straight line across reasonable ground, crossing a reedy corner just short of a fence.

Across the fence advance on the bank above the pronounced reedy ditch, approaching a wall corner with a fence corner tagged on. Keep well above the moist fence corner and resume alongside ditch and fence. Southwards are big views to Ovenden Moor windfarm beyond Haworth Moor, and also back over Watersheddles to Boulsworth Hill's crown. The path quickly improves, and as a wall comes up to take over, the way runs grandly on colourful moorland. Passing beneath the grassy hummocks of old delphs (small-scale quarry workings), a junction with the Pennine Way is reached at a wall corner on the edge of Oakworth Moor.

Turn down the wallside path, descending the moor in a straight line through several stiles and an enclosed section. Ponden Reservoir returns to the scene ahead. The path finally leaves the moor at the head of a walled grassy way winding down onto a narrow road. Go left past Crag Bottom Farm and in around the upper reaches of Dean Clough. Ignore the Pennine Way sign and remain on the road, opening out to run a level course high above the full extent of Ponden Reservoir.

Leave the road beneath a stand of windswept trees, bearing right down an enclosed bridleway. This descends to Higher Pitcher Clough Farm, and down its drive onto Oldfield Lane. Go left for only a minute, and by the seat on the bend take a gate into the field on the right (a tall fence has rendered the adjacent stile redundant). Pass left of the farmhouse below, and continue down the narrowing pasture between stream and wall. At the bottom corner cross the stream to find a stile in the fence below (not quite as per map). Turn upstream with the river Worth (a fitting conclusion) to a stile onto the road at Ponden Mill. The access road runs past the mill and ascends to the dam.

Ponden Hall

31

6

NEWSHOLME DEAN

START *Oldfield*   *Grid ref. SE 006381*

DISTANCE *8 miles (or 7 miles)*

ORDNANCE SURVEY MAPS
1:50,000
Landranger 103 - Blackburn & Burnley
Landranger 104 - Leeds, Bradford & Harrogate
1:25,000
Outdoor Leisure 21 - South Pennines

ACCESS *Start from a parking area at Hare Hill Edge above Oldfield, 200 yards west of the Grouse Inn. Oldfield is served by bus from Keighley. An alternative start is Goose Eye, mid-route.*

A walk of immense variety and colour, from the steep wooded slopes of the Dean to the wide open moor.

❺ **Begin by heading east along the road for two minutes to the** *Grouse Inn.* At exactly 1000ft up, the lounge of this popular pub makes a wonderfully sited viewpoint for the heart of Brontëland - though a little too early in this walk! **Turn off along the unsurfaced Turnshaw Road opposite the pub, which runs into a wooded corner with a seat by a modern memorial.** Set alongside a small dam, this pays tribute to the six-strong crew of a Canadian RAF Wellington bomber that tragically crashed here in January 1944.

Continue to a junction above Higher Turnshaw, and advance straight on the continuation ahead. This makes a long steady descent towards Oakworth, but is vacated after it finally swings right for the village. From a stile by a gate on the left, double back on a wallside path. A kissing-gate admits into Griff Wood, and a hollowed path runs through to the far end. Emerging at a stile, a faint path heads away, veering left over a brow. Alongside are the grassy mounds of an old quarry, while ahead are views to Newsholme and beyond.

From the brow slant down to a stile/gate onto Green Lane. Go a few yards either way and down onto Gill Lane, which dips down to re-ascend into the hamlet of Newsholme. At its heart is Church Farm, which in a fascinating architectural and spiritual arrangement stands semi-detached with a church. Linked to Oakworth parish, St. John's church was consecrated in 1840. The old farm bears a 1670 datestone, and both boast arch-headed mullioned windows.

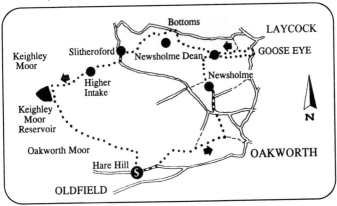

Keep straight on the road rising between the buildings. When it expires advance along the left branch, a walled grassy way straight in front. At a sharp bend leave it by the gateway in front, and a fieldside path runs on to a stile/gate high above Newsholme Dean. The path immediately undertakes a steep descent of Cat Clough. This colourful wooded cleft is our gateway into the charms of Newsholme Dean. **Head straight down, crossing the diverted stream and down through scrub to a gate. Cross to a choice of bridges on Dean Beck.** Alongside the arched farm bridge is a splendid old slab bridge, one of its four great blocks being oddly superfluous.

Across, a track heads away and slants up to the right, now enclosed, to the first of the cottages of Newsholme Dean. Follow this on past a couple more dwellings, and as it draws level with the last one it begins a more concerted climb out of the valley. At this point note the grassy track doubling back from the gate on the left: this is the onward route after the loop to incorporate Goose Eye. Omitting Goose Eye will save a good half-hour, possibly a good deal more if its hospitality were to be sampled!

The full route advances a few yards further, where go right on a narrow path above the house. Intermittently flagged, it runs through colourful terrain before dropping between old walls towards the beck. Ignoring a footbridge head downstream on the higher-level path, which soon arrives at an attractive old millpond. Just beyond it a footbridge crosses the old cut, and the path resumes in the company of the lively beck. At the end a footbridge crosses it and the path joins the road entering Goose Eye. Go left to do likewise.

Goose Eye is a former industrial hamlet sheltering in its own deep hollow, focal point very much being the popular *Turkey Inn*. It sprang into life in the late 1970s, with the opening of a tiny traditional ale brewery in an old mill building where paper for banknotes was once made. Though the venture ceased after ten years, it was revived in Keighley in 1991 much to the delight of discerning drinkers. By way of a remarkable coincidence, the pub's present owner has restored brewing to the hamlet. The confusing result is that Turkey beers are brewed in Goose Eye, and Goose Eye beers are brewed in Keighley!

Continue a short way beyond the pub, leaving by a rough access road on the left mercifully before the steep hill. Advancing past several houses on the right, the track turns sharply left up towards a lone house. Keep right on a narrower path outside its grounds, running an enclosed course around to an access road. Bear left on this, enjoying good views over the valley before it drops down to encounter the earlier route in Newsholme Dean.

Leave the access road at the first building where the gate on the right, as mentioned, sends a cart track along to another gate. Bear right on the ascending green way, and after crossing a tiny stream, remain on the upper, sunken way. This rises as a grassy track to join an old quarry track at a bend. Continue up this partly paved way, which as it swings away from the Dean reveals a Keighley Moor skyline beyond Slippery Ford. The old track emerges onto a road, Greystones Lane.

Just fifty yards along to the left, head back towards the well wooded Dean on the access road to Bottoms Farm. At the rear of the building take a small gate on the right, crossing the field bottom to a stile. Across a tiny stream the path runs round to the left, contouring the slope to where a guidepost stands in a delightful clearing. Note that the right of way has been diverted to avoid the house at Greystones just ahead, so bear left on a thin path across to a gate/stile. Now head across a couple of fields linked by wall-stiles. In the third field slant down to a gateway in the corner, and continue down to a confluence of tree-lined becks. **Cross to a gate behind, and follow the left side of the field before ascending a wallside to the farm of Slitheroford (Near Slippery Ford on maps). Pass through the gate and on between the farm buildings out onto a narrow road.**

Turn left down the road to Morkin Bridge. Leave at the parking area on a surfaced drive climbing to the house at Higher Intake. Above the house the road ascends onto moorland above the bracken-flanked clough of Morkin Beck. Passing a large isolated boulder, the heathery embankment of Keighley Moor Reservoir appears just a few minutes in front, and is quickly reached. The reservoir was constructed as far back as the 1830s to supply water to local mills, and is locally known simply as 'The Big Dam'.

Cross the embankment to a fork fifty yards beyond the end. Take the left branch, gliding gently down through the heather of Oakworth Moor, with a wide Brontë skyline in front. The moorland horizon reaches from Ovenden Moor windfarm round to Crow Hill. **Alongside an old boundary stone defaced by a modern waymark, a wall comes in for company. This is followed all the way to a wall junction as it swings left. Cross to the left side of the wall and resume along the moor edge, passing a small plantation and earning big views ahead beyond Keighley to Rombalds Moor.**

A thin path leads on to a stile in the far corner. Looking north on a clear day, distinctive Penyghent overtops various Dales heights. **Though the wall has temporarily vanished, maintain the line on a clearer path that runs to the next facing wall. Turn right on a grassy track, rising over the brow and down through heather.** Haworth appears ahead, as does Stanbury on its little ridge, with Lower Laithe and Ponden Reservoirs to either side. **Descending past a small wood sheltering a house, its drive is absorbed as the track winds down through the heather colonised quarry site of Blue Stone Delph, back onto the road at Hare Hill Edge.**

Neighbouring bridges, Newsholme Dean

35

7

WORTH VALLEY

START Haworth   Grid ref. SE 029371

DISTANCE 4½ miles

ORDNANCE SURVEY MAPS
1:50,000
Landranger 104 - Leeds, Bradford & Harrogate
1:25,000
Outdoor Leisure 21 - South Pennines

ACCESS Start from the church gates at the top of Main Street. Buses from Keighley and Bradford, and Worth Valley trains from Keighley.

Plenty of ups and downs in this exploration of some lesser known parts of the Worth Valley.

S　From the church take the short cobbled road along to the Parsonage Museum, just beyond which a footpath continues between fields and houses. It emerges to run a part-flagged course through fields to a flag-stile onto West Lane at the end of the village. Go left and immediately left again on Cemetery Road, rising onto the moorland slopes of Penistone Hill. With a pathway along the verge, there are immediately extensive views over the Worth Valley, with Lower Laithe Reservoir just ahead.

Quickly reaching a moorland cemetery, bear right down a firm track; where it leaves the moor to head towards the reservoir, instead take a grassy wallside path slanting down to the road at Dyke Farm. Turn down this road to Sladen Bridge, with its attractive cottages across. Two stone tablets set into the bridge demand a closer look, though with some caution in view of the traffic flying past. The first is a boundary stone of the long departed Haworth Urban District Council. Opposite is a more obscure tablet inscribed 'Hang On', a sober piece of advice from the days when horse-drawn coaches would have found the steep gradients somewhat challenging.

36

Across, pass along the row of cottages, and from a stile on the left climb the field to Milking Hill Farm. Pass along the front and out on its drive onto the road. Turn immediately right on the cul-de-sac lane down to the hamlet of Lumb Foot. Claiming to be twinned with the Tibetan capital, this is a very independent 'outlier' of Stanbury. **Continue down beneath the houses to a very attractive arched footbridge on the river Worth, with the remains of a mill upstream.**

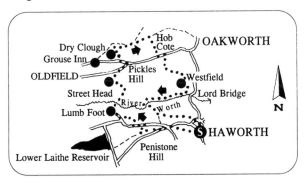

Across the little bridge a good path ascends steeply along the edge of a wooded clough. This section is particularly colourful, never more so than when decorated by springtime bluebells, or on a golden autumn day. **At a path junction at the top, go left on the old way of Street Lane.** This runs to a stile above an attractive little waterfall in a mini-ravine. A green, part sunken way rises through a newly planted strip of woodland to Street Head Farm.

Rise away on the drive, but as it merges with another, take a wall-stile on the right. Head away with the crumbling wall, and entering a smaller enclosure slant up to a gate onto Oldfield Lane, alongside Laverock Hall. This is a very attractive house of 1641: even the rear prospect which we pass is most impressive, with a battery of arch-headed mullioned windows. **Turn right past the hall to the junction at the hamlet of Pickles Hill, then double back left.**

Immediately after the last house an almost hidden path turns up a few stone steps. Ascend the fieldside with Dry Clough Farm above. When the wall turns off, slant across to a fence-stile and resume uphill alongside the colourful Dry Clough. Passing outside the farm environs to an old stile just above, scale the little bank in front and swing right along the grassy embankment. When the old dam crumbles away, advance round the part heathery bank to a wall, and go left with it. From a gap-stile at the end cross the smaller field to a gate/stile onto the unsurfaced Turnshaw Road.

Turn right on this to a junction above Higher Turnshaw, and keep straight on down the similarly rough continuation. Straight in front is the village of Oakworth, with Rombalds Moor on the skyline behind. **Leave after 250 yards, alongside a covered reservoir. From a gate on the right descend to the house at Turnshaw, passing through stiles to its left and out along the drive onto Hob Cote Lane.**

Go left for about 150 yards along the road to the third drive on the right, identified by distinctive gateposts. Follow this past a house and down to Green Well. This spell enjoys a great Worth Valley prospect, from Haworth around to Withins Height. **Pass left of the farm, through an untidy corner and straight down an improving green way. From a stile on the left at the bottom, cross two fields and slant down to a superior stile in the corner.** Almost lost in the grass hereabouts are sections of flagged path. **Follow the wall away, taking a stile half way along to descend to Westfield Farm.**

Cross straight over its drive to a small gate, and resume a stepped descent to join another track. Just below it is a stile from where the river Worth leads upstream. Although the right of way cuts out three diminishing loops of the river, the first, larger one can be traced if the Countryside Stewardship scheme is still operating. This is a lovely section on the deep dale floor, with herons and dippers in regular attendance.

Long Bridge,
River Worth

A small weir is passed to meet the foot of the wooded bank. Squeezing through here, ignore a fence-stile that regains the river, and keep straight on the base of the bank. Emerging from the trees and scrub to a wall-stile ahead, continue on again to regain the returning riverbank. Through a wide gap in the wall, again ignore a stile on the left: though a well tramped path stays with the river, beyond the next bend it has no escape from confinement between river and barbed fence. Remain outside the fence and on through a gate/stile, then on again past a pond to a ladder-stile.

Beyond this point simply shadow the Worth upstream for the few minutes to where it swings sharply round to Long Bridge. This shapely, stone arched footbridge is the focal point of our crossing of the Worth Valley by this old packhorse route. The narrow bridge hovers over a confluence of the river Worth and Sladen Beck, while beneath it is a ford. Though harnessed to supply numerous mills in times past, the Worth largely avoids human contact until skirting the edge of Keighley before joining the Aire.

Cross the bridge and follow the path climbing away, initially above Sladen Beck, to a stile. The old way regains its sunken nature to climb between long crumbled walls, but part way up spoils itself and it is necessary to escape into the field edge. A ladder-stile at the top admits to the environs of a house, Lower Oldfield Farm. Go left in front of it, through a tiny snicket and then across a field top to a stile in the fence opposite. Stay with the right-hand wall to a gate/stile from where an enclosed way heads away. The continuing path runs along the base of a patch of open ground, becoming enclosed and passing between graveyards to emerge into Haworth. Go left and then quickly right to re-enter the main street by way of Changegate.

Laverock Hall

8

BROW MOOR

START *Haworth*   *Grid ref. SE 034372*

DISTANCE *5½ miles*

ORDNANCE SURVEY MAPS
1:50,000
Landranger 104 - Leeds, Bradford & Harrogate
1:25,000
Outdoor Leisure 21 - South Pennines

ACCESS *Start from Haworth station on the Keighley & Worth Valley line. Station car park and other nearby parking. Keighley-Oxenhope trains at summer and weekends all year; buses from Keighley.*

Beckside and moorland walking within a stone's throw of Haworth, often enlivened by the sight, sound and smell of steam trains.

❺   Haworth station is home of the Keighley & Worth Valley Railway. The 5-mile cul-de-sac line from Keighley was closed to passengers at the end of 1961, and six months later freight services were withdrawn. Already, however, enthusiasts had formed a preservation society, and in 1968 the line triumphantly re-opened at the dawn of independently preserved steam railways. Though short in length it is one of the finest and friendliest of such lines, with stations at Keighley, Ingrow, Damems, Oakworth, Haworth and Oxenhope. It has been a location for numerous film and television projects, but it was the making of the classic family film *The Railway Children* that earned the 'Worth Valley' a lasting fame. Another claim to fame is the operation of a buffet car purveying real beer, which has earned the KWVR a unique 'mobile' entry in the Good Beer Guide!
    From the station forecourt cross the footbridge over the line, and turn left on Belle Isle Road, joining Bridgehouse Lane. Go left on the road bridge over the railway (with a view into the often busy yard) and bear immediately right on Brow Road. This immediately

swings left to start climbing, but leave it just as quickly by taking a few steps up to a stile on the right. A flagged path heads away, along the field bottom to join the long-drained course of a former mill-cut. Almost at once the bustle of Haworth is behind, and all is green. Over to the right the railway runs parallel across Bridgehouse Beck. Up above hover the flapping sails of the Brow Moor wind turbine, first in the area in 1992.

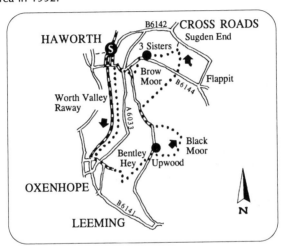

Before long the path bridges the old cut and runs on with it to its termination, where the path forks. One branch drops down to a footbridge on the now adjacent beck, while ours runs straight ahead (featuring some old flagging) to an old house. Take a stile opposite and cross the field bottom to a gate into a garden. Pass along the front of the house, and at the gate as the drive heads away, the path turns down to the right to rejoin the beck. Just a little further it passes a lovely stone arched bridge.

Don't cross but continue pleasantly upstream to cross at a purely functional footbridge. The way resumes upstream past a solitary house and out on a drive. When it bridges the beck, remain on the near side on a path sandwiched between beck and railway. At another footbridge recross the beck and the path runs along to emerge into a former mill yard and out onto Harry Lane on the edge of Oxenhope, with the station just down to the right (see page 20).

The walk turns left up Harry Lane onto the A6033 Keighley-Hebden Bridge road. Cross straight over and up the steep Dark Lane to its demise into a rough track beyond the lone Lower Croft House. Narrowing, it levels out to reach a ruined substantial farm, sad yet very photogenic. From here there are big views over Oxenhope village, in its basin amid steep hills rising to long moorland skylines. Here leave the track by doubling back on a short-lived green way to a stile onto the base of the heathery bank of Bentley Hey.

A slender path begins a steady ascent half-left, tracing the line of a sunken way through some enthusiastic gorse. It gradually scales a tiny heather ridge before a longer level section across open country. This provides some lovely views across the valley, possibly with steam trains chugging away far below. Approaching the end, the sunken way and gorse return to resume the slant uphill to a stile/gateway onto Black Moor Road. On a clear day, look far to the north-west to see, above Oakworth Moor, the shapely outlines of both Ingleborough and Penyghent, some 28 miles distant.

The direct route goes left along this quiet back road for three-quarters of a mile, though a detour onto the edge of Black Moor adds an extra quarter-hour's interest. For this, almost immediately turn right along a rough road past Upwood caravan site. Massive views ahead feature Rombalds Moor, Almscliff Crag, Otley Chevin and Baildon Moor, while to the north are the Yorkshire Dales heights of Great Whernside, Meugher and Simon's Seat above Wharfedale. The lane expires at a bridle-gate onto heathery Black Moor. While the main path runs straight ahead, turn left on a grassy wallside path, declining very gently to another broad track joining the moor. Pass through the gate onto this similar walled way (Cuckoo Park Lane) back out to rejoin Black Moor Road.

Turning right, the windpump re-appears just ahead now. Immediately before the quarry it overlooks, a broad path turns up the wallside onto Brow Moor. This soon improves as it shadows the sturdy wall over the heathery brow and along to Brow Top Road (B6144). Ahead are good views to Rombalds Moor and the Aire Valley beyond Keighley, and also back over the upper reaches of the Worth Valley to Pendle Hill peeking over Watersheddles.

Cross straight over and down the rough road of Hardgate Lane, which beyond Hardgate Cottage becomes no more than a footway. Descending past old quarries, it becomes a rough road again at another house. Here take a stile on the left and cross the field bottom towards a small reservoir. Entering a heathery bank, a good path slants up to a wall then contours through the heather to a sudden arrival at the *Three Sisters* pub. No prizes are offered for guessing the identity of the sisters in question at this modern establishment. Its drive leads back up onto Brow Top Road.

Go right for just fifty yards to the Haworth/30mph signs. Haworth itself returns to the scene, as does the ubiquitous wind turbine. Here a good path heads off across Brow Moor, angling very gently down back onto Black Moor Road. Turn right a few yards then a path cuts a corner to drop back down onto Brow Top Road. Just below is Hebden Road (A6033), beneath which the extremely steep Brow Road winds down through Haworth Brow into Haworth. Go straight over the railway bridge and up Bridgehouse Lane for the village centre, or turn right along Station Road for the station, not surprisingly.

Main Street,
Haworth

9

HAWORTH MOOR

START Haworth   Grid ref. SE 029371

DISTANCE 7½ miles

ORDNANCE SURVEY MAPS
1:50,000
Landranger 103 - Blackburn & Burnley
Landranger 104 - Leeds, Bradford & Harrogate
1:25,000
Outdoor Leisure 21 - South Pennines

ACCESS Start from the church gates at the top of Main Street. Buses from Keighley and Bradford, and Worth Valley trains from Keighley.

A rich and varied ramble to the south-west of Haworth, its famous heather moor being just one of many interesting features.

❺ **From the front of the church, leave the Main Street by the flagged path to the left across the churchyard. It leaves by an iron kissing-gate and rises past allotments. At a T-junction above the car park turn right up a broader way, rising past the house at Balcony to emerge onto Dimples Lane on the edge of Penistone Hill. Cross straight over and bear left on the signposted path through the heather.**

Penistone Hill has changed from man's workshop to his playground. It is designated a country park, its former quarries now put to use as car parks for the leisure seeker. With its grand views of the Worth Valley and the heather moors beyond, this is as far as most visitors will venture. Most of the numerous guideposts over the next hour or so feature Japanese, an indication of the fascination for the Brontës with students from the Land of the Rising Sun. More sceptical observers see it as merely a gimmick that has earned extensive publicity for the area!

Good views look over the valley to the settlements of Oldfield, Pickles Hill and Oakworth, and back over Keighley to Rombalds Moor. The Brontë moorlands increasingly feature ahead, from Withins Height round above Stanbury to Wycoller Ark. **Running broadly on, keep right at a signposted fork (both pointing to Brontë Falls!) and the main path runs on towards old quarry spoil at the far end, culminating in a parking area.** The more distant Ponden Reservoir is joined by Lower Laithe Reservoir, just ahead, with Stanbury village behind it. Note the parallel wall patterns dropping from village to reservoir. Stanbury stands on the crest of a ridge between Sladen Beck and the Worth Valley, making it easily identified in local views.

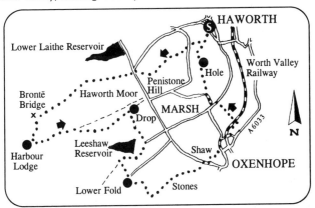

Keep right here, and very quickly a branch path (still the Brontë Way) is signed down to the right at a track junction, slanting down to cross unfenced Moorside Lane. Just up to the left, on the brow is Tom Stell's Seat, its hoary gritstone inscribed with the name of a local rambler 'who loved these moors'. **The path continues across the road, winding down to join a rough road at a cattle-grid. Turn left on this to march along the edge of Haworth Moor.** Haworth Moor is part of the South Pennine Moors Site of Special Scientific Interest, and is internationally renowned for its breeding birds.

The rough road runs unfailingly on above abandoned farms in the fields below. Lower Laithe Reservoir was the culprit, as water boards cleared folk from the land to avoid contamination. **The way narrows into a broad path as the moor opens out.** The isolated farmstead of Harbour Lodge is seen ahead, but more stirring is the Top

Withins skyline, attendant trees aiding identification as it just breaks the horizon. **Across to the right is the colourful side valley of South Dean Beck, into which the walk is about to descend. The rougher path runs down and on to arrive at Brontë Bridge.** This an attractive clapper-type bridge on the main route to Top Withins. By the path immediately before it is the stone known for obvious reasons as the Brontë Chair, while another boulder carries a brass plaque with a biblical quote. A boulder by the bridge bears a stone tablet recording its re-building in 1990 following flash floods.

The Brontë Bridge

Instead of crossing the bridge, take the rougher path climbing up the west bank of the sidestream boasting the equally famed Brontë Waterfall. This slender trickle no different from a thousand other tinkling Pennine streams surely pushes the literary connection a little too far! **This rough climb quickly levels out and the path runs on towards the isolated farm of Harbour Lodge. Passing grouse butts, the path runs to a small footbridge, above which is the access road.** Just above is a memorial to a former gamekeeper of these moors.

Turn left away from the farm, and on for some time until beyond an appreciable kink. As the road levels and straightens, it is seen for some distance ahead as it crosses the moor. Locating a thin path slanting off to the right, this angles down, initially moistly, to improve tenfold before reaching a wall along the bottom of the moor. A good path is joined to run along to the left. After a gentle rise Penistone Hill re-appears ahead, with Drop Farm (refreshments) just ahead. For a direct return to Haworth keep straight on past Drop to the road, and back over the crest of Penistone Hill.

Without approaching Drop Farm, take a stile in the kink of the wall and head away down the fieldside, with Leeshaw Reservoir just below. At the foot of a second field Westfield Farm is reached, and its drive leads down onto the end of Lee Lane. Turn right, losing its surface to pass beneath the grassy dam and then climbing up above

the reservoir as Bodkin Lane. Well before Bodkin Farm, take a gate on the left and cross the fieldtop to a corner stile, then diagonally across the next field up to a stile. At the other end of this small enclosure a stile empties onto a sharp bend of Outside Lane.

Advance straight on the short way to Lower Fold. Behind the first house is a track junction. Go left round the rear of the house, and at the farm entrance an enclosed footway sets off to its left. With some fine sections of intermittent paving, this walled way winds down into Rag Clough, climbing back out and along to the foot of the pocket moorland of Stones. This is a prominent, locally popular heathery island surrounded by green pastures.

Follow this broad way the length of the base of Stones. Passing the house at Far Stones Farm, it turns down into Stone Lane to drop steeply past cottages onto Shaw Lane on the edge of Oxenhope. Turn right for just 100 yards, then take a short drive to the attractive Shaw Farm on the left. Pass right of the house, into a little shrubbery before an enclosed path escapes. Quickly leading to a stile, cross the field to a gate into sports fields. Join the firm path across the grass, which winds left around to emerge onto Cross Lane. Turn down this to a junction, and right along Mill Lane to the railway station.

Oxenhope's best connection with Haworth is the Keighley & Worth Valley Railway. This is the line's terminus, with a new museum opened in 2001 (see page 40 for more on the KWVR). Across the road is the Millennium Green. For more on Oxenhope please see page 20. From the station entrance go straight ahead along Mill Lane, and as it quickly becomes Harry Lane, turn left along a rough road. This soon ends at a house with a stone inscription above the door. An inviting footpath takes over, running alongside Bridgehouse Beck to a footbridge. Across it, turn up onto the railway. Cross with care to a path slanting left up to a stile in the wall above. Climb the wallside to the houses, emerging via a gate/gap into the yard. That on the left is Bents House, which featured as 'Three Chimneys', home of the Railway Children in the classic film.

Head directly away on the straight drive that emerges onto Marsh Lane in the scattered hamlet of Marsh. Turn left, briefly, then first right up Old Oxenhope Lane. The house on the corner here is Marshlands - Arthur Bell Nichols stayed here before his marriage to Charlotte Brontë in 1854. Note the attractive facade of Old Oxenhope Hall hidden in foliage on the left. At the bend at the top step into the yard at the rear of Old Oxenhope Farm, then left up the wallside away. Over the wall is an old millpond.

Sections of old causey protrude as the way joins a farm track through a gate/stile and rises to the brow. Here locate a stile on the left admitting to a narrow, short-lived enclosed green footway. At the end resume on the left side of the wall. Ahead is a big view down the length of the Worth Valley, with Oakworth to the left and Haworth Brow nearer to hand. Intriguingly, Haworth itself stays cleverly hidden from view. At the far end of the Worth Valley are the houses of Riddlesden beneath Rivock Edge and the Rombalds Moor skyline. Across to the right is the solitary wind turbine overlooking a large sandstone quarry, while directly behind us many of the Ovenden Moor brethren are now breaking the skyline.

Keep on to reach Hole Farm, with its modern additions alongside. As the drive turns left to climb away, take the left of two stiles on the right, and head across the field again towards Sowdens House at the end. The siting of a modern urban street light in the field here will arouse curiosity: note also the sundial on the house side. **The path turns into a narrow snicket to descend and zigzag along to rejoin the outward route at the junction of ways above the car park. Amazingly, despite its apparent absence, the heart of the village is just two minutes ahead. Conclude the walk on the cobbles and flags on which it began, to re-enter the churchyard.**

St. Michael's, Haworth

48

10

KELBROOK MOOR

START *Foulridge*   *Grid ref. SD 888426*

DISTANCE *7 miles*

ORDNANCE SURVEY MAPS
1:50,000
Landranger 103 - Blackburn & Burnley
1:25,000
Outdoor Leisure 21 - South Pennines

ACCESS *Start from Foulridge Wharf, just off the B6251, itself just off the A56. Car park. Served by Skipton-Colne/Burnley buses.*

A splendid contrast of gentle hills and canal towpath.

⑤   Foulridge is a small village astride the Colne-Skipton road, and in areal extent is overshadowed by the adjacent reservoir. This was constructed to supply the Leeds-Liverpool Canal, which at this point runs north to Salterforth (the final leg of the walk). Foulridge Wharf was an integral part of the waterway in its commercial heyday: the surviving warehouse still carries the paintwork of *Leeds & Liverpool Canal Company General Carriers*. The moorings host a colourful array of boats, public cruises and a tearoom. Here the canal enters the mile-long Foulridge Tunnel: from here locks are downhill in both directions. The entrance is just 100 yards distant: boaters' passage through is controlled by traffic lights. By the car park is a 200-year old kiln where lime was brought to produce mortar used in construction of the locks, bridges, reservoirs and the tunnel itself.

From the Wharf head back up the access road, joining another road and up a few yards further to the *Hole in the Wall* pub. Turn left here on Town Gate, to a sloping green. This is a very attractive backwater, with rows of small cottages lining its top side. **Rise past the Post office/shop to Towngate Steps onto the main road (A56).** Along to the right are two further pubs, the *New Inn* and the *Hare & Hounds*.

Cross and ascend the narrow Stoney Lane. At the top go right a few yards, then left up a corner of a tiny green. **Advance just a few yards up this back road, and take a snicket on the left between houses. This runs a tight course between gardens to emerge into a field.**

Bear left up the field, maintaining a straight line cutting through several further fields. After a couple of fence-stiles a sturdy wall-stile waits in a corner. From a gateway in the next wall, rise left to a wall-stile on the brow, with a few scattered rocks around. Already there are excellent views, looking beyond Foulridge and its lower reservoir to Burn Moor and White Moor, and northwards up the valley to an array of Yorkshire Dales heights. **Turn right with the wall, through a collapsed wall with a shapely knoll above.** This is the site of an old quarry with a communications mast close by. **The path contours round its left side to a stile in the wall ahead. Through this ascend the wallside onto Noyna Hill.**

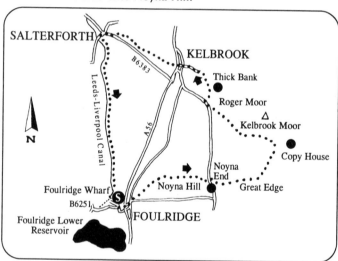

Simply remain with the wall onto Noyna Hill's broad top. The highest point is a modest 985ft/300m, just further along. Pendle Hill looms large over Burn Moor, while the massive Dales skyline includes Ingleborough and Great Whernside. More relevant to our walk are the heathery tract of Kelbrook Moor and the insignificant Great Edge ahead, while Boulsworth Hill reveals its mighty frame to the south-east. A slight rise follows an intervening stile, and towards the end take a stile on the right. The path runs enclosed for 50 yards by animal pens. Emerging, slant left down to a fence-stile, then bear right with the fence down to a stile onto the narrow back road of Cob Lane, alongside the house at Noyna End.

Go right just past the house, and take a gate on the left. A grassy track doubles back across the field, but is left within a hundred yards by turning right, down to a footbridge on a tiny stream. A neat little path slants up the bank, then downstream towards a wall ahead. Don't pass through the gate, but turn up the near side, steeply to a ladder-stile in the wall at the top. Continue rising with a fence, a concerted haul up the reedy tract of Great Edge. Pausing to look back, Foulridge's reservoirs occupy the valley bottom, with Pendle Hill and the Bowland moors leading northwards round to Yorkshire's Three Peaks.

At the top veer right to a ladder-stile in the wall above. Head away with the wall as far as a ladder-stile in it, just short of the highest point. Across to the right, Boulsworth Hill now forms a vast skyline. Bear left across the field to a fence-stile near the corner, then turn right alongside some greenery to a wall-stile. Bear left to join a farm track, passing through a gateway to the corner ahead. Don't use the gate, but take the ladder-stile onto a corner of Kelbrook Moor.

Head directly away, with only traces of a path but on an obvious line aiming for the top side of the cluster of trees ahead. To the right a vast sweep of heather rises to the Ordnance Survey column crowning the moor at 1178ft/359m. A pleasant stride through the heather continues to a second similar stand of trees. Stunning views look across to a long Bowland skyline sandwiched between Pendle Hill with its supporting moors, and Ingleborough with its greater supporting cast. Beyond these trees bear left, slanting down the moor to a corner where fence and wall meet. It is easy to me misled by a clearer path (not the route of the right of way) running across to a small gateway in the wall ahead, which could then be followed down to the bottom corner.

Pass through the gateway and resume down the heathery Roger Moor. This section will delight devotees of James Bond or the Saint, the rest can continue to savour the panoramic views over Lancashire and Yorkshire. Preferably keep a little above the wall to avoid the worst of some moist moments part way down. On approaching Hard Clough Farm over the wall, contour round to the right through the heathery hummocks of an old quarry. This avoids a cul-de-sac corner, to find another wall corner in front. From it follow the wall just a little further down to a ladder-stile in a small corner. Leave the moor and descend the field to a stile back onto Cob Lane, at a junction with a farm road.

Turn down this for a minute as far as a drive on the right. Turn on this until just past the house, where an enclosed path runs around the edge of the garden into a field. Drop down to the wall heading away, quickly taking a stile to resume on the other side of the tiny watercourse and fence. With the houses of Kelbrook below, enjoy a pleasant descent alongside the tiny stream, which sinks underground at the bottom. Bear right to a gate/stile and descend the pasture, passing the reborn stream to a gate/stile in front of the houses below. Between these bear left down the access road, and straight on through to the Main Street. To the right stands the church of St. Mary the Virgin, dating from 1839.

Advance straight on the short Vicarage Road to the main road (A56) directly ahead. Kelbrook's various services include a chippy just to the left, and the *Craven Heifer* opposite. Cross straight over to the rough road alongside the pub. After passing a house an enclosed footway takes over, past the village team's football pitch. Ending at a stile into a field, head directly away with a hedge on the right. A stile at the end sends steps down onto an old railway cutting. This is the late, lamented course of the Skipton-Colne line. Opened in 1849 the railway was once a vital Yorkshire-Lancashire link, and though it narrowly survived the Beeching cuts, its closure in 1970 left Colne a cul-de-sac and Skipton no longer a junction.

Bear right a few yards and then out the other side via another stile. Head away again, quickly crossing a stile in the fence to resume on the other side. This stage to Salterforth is overshadowed by the noise of the parallel road. Crossing a drain by a small footbridge resume directly away, quickly onto an embanked path. This slavishly shadows a watercourse all the way to Salterforth. Towards the end it becomes enclosed before emerging onto the main road to Barnoldswick (B6383).

Cross the road a little further along and turn up Salterforth Lane to the *Anchor Inn,* alongside the Leeds-Liverpool Canal. This celebrated pub dates back several centuries, and was astride an old salt way, a regular halt in packhorse times. Transported all over the north from mines in Cheshire, salt was important for preserving meat, and indeed it gave the village its name from the simple translation of 'salters' ford'. The original pub, the Travellers Rest, was in fact at a lower level, but construction of the canal made a higher level building necessary. The pub is also renowned for its cellar, which features stalactite formations as a result of its damp situation beneath the canal. Opposite the pub are Salterforth Moorings.

The Anchor Inn, Salterforth

Join the towpath alongside the pub and head south, the waterway leading unfailingly back for a lengthy stride of virtually two miles to Foulridge Wharf. The canal runs a 127¼ mile course between its two great city termini, and is the northernmost of three trans-Pennine waterways. The canal engineers took advantage of the low-level Aire Gap to breach the Pennines by way of a chain of locks, only resorting to tunneling here at Foulridge. Begun in 1770 and fully opened in 1816 for what proved to be a short-lived industrial use, it was swiftly overtaken by the arrival of the railways. Today it is a vibrant leisure amenity, for walkers, bargees, anglers, naturalists, and in places, cyclists.

This section is a lovely stroll in untainted, rural surroundings as good as any length of the canal. Features of interest include a colourful moorings, open views across to Kelbrook Moor and Noyna Hill, the true county boundary marked by signs at a stone-arched bridge, which also shelters a milestone (Leeds 44¼, Liverpool 83), and the possibility of glimpsing a kingfisher. Approaching the end, the embankment of the old railway is very prominent to the left: it stops suddenly at the point where it bridged the canal.

11

WYCOLLER DEAN

START *Wycoller*　　　　*Grid ref. SD 926394*

DISTANCE *6¼ miles*

ORDNANCE SURVEY MAPS
1:50,000
Landranger 103 - Blackburn & Burnley
1:25,000
Outdoor Leisure 21 - South Pennines

ACCESS *Start from the main village car park, on a cul-de-sac road off the Colne-Trawden road at Cottontree, reached from Trawden or from Laneshaw Bridge. Mileage is measured from the car park.*

Easy walking to visit many interesting features of the Wycoller valley.

⑤ **From the car park a roadside footway runs on to the edge of Wycoller.** This fascinating hamlet of mullioned windowed cottages was by-passed by the outside world since the Industrial Revolution failed to gain a foothold. It is difficult to believe that two centuries ago, several hundred people lived here. Handloom weaving was a major industry, but as the large mills sprang up, workers abandoned the place to take up employment in the towns. As a result Wycoller spent much of the 20th century largely derelict, but more recently its very isolation and untouched character have ensured it popularity.

　　Today Wycoller has its own country park administered by the Lancashire Countryside Service, visitors flock here, and all but the hall seems to be renovated. In open space stand the ruins of Wycoller Hall, a 16th century country house later extended by the last squire, Henry Cunliffe. It is thought to have been the Ferndean Manor of Charlotte Brontë's *Jane Eyre*. Alongside is an ancient clapper bridge, while a most characterful packhorse bridge of 13th century origin stands by a ford. The restored Aisled Barn was built in the 1630s to store grain, and was later used as a carriage house. Along with the old hall it is the focal point, and features a display including the area's weaving history. There is also a craft centre and refreshments. Pepper Hill Barn is the main information and study centre, just up the slope.

To leave Wycoller, cross the packhorse bridge to the hall. Stone steps climb the grassy bank behind, and at the top a broad path rises up the field. If followed all the way it leads to the Haworth Road car park, an alternative start point. Alongside the path is a good example of vaccary walling, an old style of field boundary consisting of upright slabs (a vaccary was a cattle farm). **Approaching a deep sunken section, go right to a stile and a cross a couple of fields. After the next stile the path forks, and here opt for the one slanting up to the left.** Further vaccary walling is evident all around.

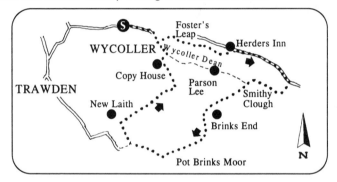

Passing through a collapsed wall, Foster's Leap appears ahead. Continue up to a wall corner with a stile just beyond, from where the wall leads away to a farm road. Cross straight over to reach the rocks of Foster's Leap. Head along the top of the outcrops, soon with an accompanying wall which continues well beyond the rocks. The way remains with the 'edge' longer than the map suggests: with the *Herders Inn* **appearing just ahead, make a short drop to a stile in the wall. Through it rise half-left to a barn, and small gates to its left lead into the pub car park.**

Turn right on the road for almost three-quarters of a mile as it traverses the edge of rough moorland. Ahead is a brief glimpse of the aptly named Watersheddles Reservoir, with the Wolf Stones on the moorland skyline to the left. **After the last buildings it swings sharply left, and just beyond this turn down an initially enclosed byway into the head of Smithy Clough, with Boulsworth Hill rising ahead.**

*Boulsworth Hill
from Foster's Leap*

The rough road runs unfailingly down, crossing the stream by a stone arched bridge in the environs of the extensive grassy mounds of **Smithy Clough Scar, also known as Hilly Holes.** These hushings result from centuries-old limestone extraction. The boulders were won by releasing water from dams formed by diverted streams, scouring vegetation away in the process. The stone would be fired in kilns, and the resulting powder was commonly used as a sweetener for spreading on acidic moorland soils to improve them for cultivation.

Glorious views stretch far out over Pendle country to the big hill itself. Back over to the right the *Herders* perches above the rocky bank of Foster's Leap. **The track swings up to a brow and junction where Brontë Way and Pendle Way meet.** For an easy finish, pass through the stile and descend the track to Parson Lee Farm, whose drive becomes a traffic-free byway in tandem with the stream. This arrangement is maintained through Wycoller Dean back to the start.

The main route continues along the track, though don't march blindly off along its obvious course. Instead, after 100 yards bear right on a reedy wallside path. Beyond a gate in the corner it runs on more happily along the field top, becoming briefly enclosed before emerging into true open country beneath Brink Ends, a gaunt looking place. Between diverging walls keep straight on, descending to a gate in a wall before crossing the deep Turnhole Clough. Up the other bank an old boundary stone is passed as the path rises gently away, upstream through increasingly colourful terrain. The many contours of Boulsworth Hill now entirely dominate this fine surround of rolling moorland. Sections of stone causey testify to the history of this old packhorse route: several of them incorporate benchmarks.

In the company of little Saucer Hill Clough, a lengthy section with a sturdy wall leads to the brow of the hill, and the path descends to a junction with an access road. Turn right on this, over the cattle-grid off the moor and through a field. Absorbing a farm drive it drops down to become enclosed at the cottage at Mean Moss. Leave the road here, and pass along the front of the house to a stile in front of some garages. Resume across the field to a fine wall-stile, and on through two further fields in the company of a wall.

The end stile is reached with New Laith Farm just across the field in front. Don't advance to it, but turn right on the wallside. Just short of the corner, a stile at a massive gatepost admits to a corner of rough pasture. Go left through the gate onto a walled way. At the end, advance straight on with a reedy ditch down to a novel stile by a gate. Directly in front are the features of the walk's earlier stages. Cross to a corner stile and down to another into rougher pasture. Follow the crumbling right-hand wall away as it curves around to a sturdy wall. Just fifty yards down this is a stile, and just below that a bridle-gate. Wycoller Dean is now well revealed, with both its dalehead farms seen beneath Foster's Leap and the moorland slopes.

Descend with the wall, and stay with it as it swings down to the left. Before the bottom corner cross the wall at a stile/gate, and from a step-stile behind, resume down the other side past a wood. At the bottom corner go left just a few yards to a wall-stile, then cross to the farm buildings at Copy House. Passing through two gates turn right in front of the buildings, and as the track heads away, take a stile on the right to descend the wallside to Wycoller Beck. Either cross the small bridge to the rough road to go left and finish, or use the path on this side, downstream by some ponds to enter the hamlet.

Wycoller Hall

12

BOULSWORTH HILL

START *Trawden*   *Grid ref. SD 911386*

DISTANCE *5¾ miles*

ORDNANCE SURVEY MAPS
1:50,000
Landranger 103 - Blackburn & Burnley
1:25,000
Outdoor Leisure 21 - South Pennines

ACCESS *Start from the church at the central crossroads. Roadside parking nearby. Served by bus from Colne.*

A clear day is strongly recommended for this straightforward ascent of a supreme viewpoint.

S Trawden is a village outlier of Colne, easternmost of the Lancashire mill towns. Trawden's affinity with Boulsworth Hill is, in its own way, akin to the Horton/Penyghent and Fort William/Ben Nevis partnerships (honest!). It has a couple of pubs, and a tearoom at the Hollin Hall sewing centre. **Take the long cul-de-sac road south-east from the crossroads by the church, which runs for a good half mile between houses to the sewing centre at the mill at Hollin Hall.** Ahead, Boulsworth Hill forms an imposing and inviting skyline.

Leaving the village the way narrows into a country road, which is followed until a sharp bend left. Go straight ahead along a farm road, keeping left of the buildings to a bridle-gate at the far end of the farmyard. A track runs on to another gate, then descends to cross a small tree-lined stream. A tiny detour down the opposite bank reveals a vantage point for the shady hollow enclosing the waterfall of Lumb Spout. The cottage named on the map is a pile of rubble.

From the beck head directly away up a prominent dry groove to a scattering of trees, a little beyond which is a stile. Continue up the wallside behind to rise gently onto a rough access road on the

base of the open moor. **Turn right just fifty yards on this towards the barns at Spoutley Lumb, then go left up a concrete waterworks access road to begin the ascent proper of Boulsworth Hill. The full circuit is enjoyed on a looping, elongated horseshoe concession path. The climb to the summit is a splendidly invigorating one, infusing a real sense of actually climbing a hill.**

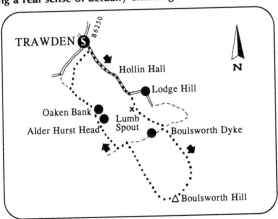

The easy surface is soon relinquished as the path forges uphill, marker posts confirming the obvious route. Beyond an early kissing-gate in a fence, the path narrows and enjoys a steep section. When this eases the summit is revealed further to the right. Gentler slopes lead up to the Little Chair Stones, and the sometimes fainter and sometimes moist path swings right to slant up to the skyline Weather Stones. This cluster is the best on the walk, featuring some massive boulders. From here the rolling moors stretch eastwards across the Pennine watershed to Crow Hill and Withins Height above the head of Walshaw Dean. **A two minute walk south-west across the broad top leads to the waiting Ordnance Survey column.**

Boulsworth Hill rises as an upturned boat from the rolling moorland, and its lengthy top bristles with an assortment of gritstone outcrops. The summit, Lad Law, is itself a cluster of boulders, and at 1696ft/517m this is one of the principal summits of the South Pennines. Our moorland spell above the intake wall is enjoyed courtesy of the water company, which has deigned to allow the public a narrow access strip. Don't forget to pay those water rates! Boulsworth's greatest asset as a viewpoint is its 360° panorama. A good half-hour could be passed identifying the many hills and moors, which include those of the Yorkshire Dales, the Lake District, Bowland and the Peak District.

Boulsworth Hill summit, looking west to Pendle Hill

Return on a path heading west, initially moist but quickly reaching a scattering of boulders around the upright Abbot Stone. From this fine location the ground steepens, and the path transforms into a grassy, surprisingly peat-free way. Beyond a fence-stile the last stage accompanies a wall down to rejoin the rough road by way of some moister moments. Go left on this, over a minor brow and down to cross **Will Moor Clough.** Part way up the other side leave the track by a gate/stile on the right, from where a rough track heads away past a derelict barn at Antley Gate. At another gate/stile the way runs on between fences to a wall-stile in a moist corner at the end. Improving now, the way continues along a wallside to the house at **Alder Hurst Head.**

From the corner gate pass left of the house on a green way, continuing straight on to a gate at the head of a small wooded clough. From here a short-lived walled way descends to a cart track above a cluster of buildings at Oaken Bank. Turn left on this, across the stream. It heads away alongside a wall, then climbs steeply to a **gate.** This is worth leaning on to look back at Boulsworth towering beyond the mini-hamlet at our feet. **The way then eases to run on past two isolated houses.**

Just past the second house (Pasture Springs), take a slim stile in the fence on the right and head away with the wall towards a mast on its other side. Continue beyond a corner stile nearer the mast, descending to another wall corner below. By now Trawden has been fully revealed directly below. **Slant left to join the descending wall, and ignoring the stile in it, resume down the final two fields. In the corner just before the bottom, a tiny gate admits to a short-lived snicket emerging onto an urban street. Follow this down onto the road, with the church junction just along to the left.**

Lumb Spout

```
┌─────────────────────────────┐
│            ( 13 )           │
│                             │
│        WEETS HILL           │
└─────────────────────────────┘
```

START *Barnoldswick*   *Grid ref. SD 879466*

DISTANCE *7¼ miles*

ORDNANCE SURVEY MAPS
1:50,000
Landranger 103 - Blackburn & Burnley
1:25,000
Outdoor Leisure 21 - South Pennines **or**
Outdoor Leisure 41 - Forest of Bowland & Ribblesdale

ACCESS *Start from the Tourist Information Centre, alongside the Post office on Fernlea Avenue. Across the road is Wellhouse Road car park. Served by Skipton-Colne/Burnley buses.*

An invigorating tramp over the Barnoldswick heights, with glorious views from Weets Hill and heather surrounds on White Moor.

S Barnoldswick, along with neighbouring Earby, is a part of Yorkshire gone temporarily missing after the 1974 boundary revisions, though as these are strictly local government changes, it is generally accepted as still being part of real Yorkshire. Known locally as 'Barlick', this independent little town is something of a backwater between Skipton and Colne, yet boasts a wide range of services for its size: the modern Town Square is an attractive focal point. Barnoldswick grew with the cotton industry, which saw its population treble during the early part of the 20th century. Sadly the 1980s witnessed the final demise of weaving, though two very large employers ensure this is a very important site of local employment.

The car park opposite the Post office is the site of the town's former railway station, opened in 1871. The last train left here in September 1965. **From the TIC head away along the short Station Road, and continue along the shop-lined Church Street (B6251) at the end. Dropping down between the *Seven Stars* and the *Cross***

Keys, **bear right along Walmsgate.** An imposing Independent Methodist Church of 1892 stands on the left. **Follow the road uphill to Town Head, continuing round to the left as Westgate.** This corner features some attractive buildings: on the right is Quaker House, bearing an oval tablet inscribed *Built by the Barnoldswick Friendly Society AD 1829.*

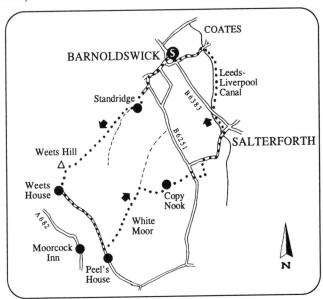

With Bancroft mill chimney in view just ahead, turn right along suburban Moorgate Road. Bancroft Mill was the last of Barnoldswick's many mills to be built, and began weaving cotton in 1920. It is home to a rare steam engine which operated for more than half a century. The engine house survives, with its tall, circular red-brick chimney alongside. A trust now preserves the engine which draws visitors when in operation on certain days. **Moorgate Road quickly ends on the edge of modern suburbia: head up the continuing narrow Folly Lane, which soon zigzags steeply uphill.** A pause is merited, and probably needed, to appraise a fine view back over the town, backed by a wide sweep of Yorkshire Dales hills including Great Whernside.

Just past the lone Standridge Farm, take a stile by a gate on the right and resume up the fieldside. This grand uphill stride maintains its course when the parallel lane turns off. Simply continue uphill all the way, passing through several stiles as the terrain changes to rougher grassy moorland above a colourful steep bank. The steeper work is accomplished to leave a very gentle stride, and through the final stile a crumbling circular pillar stands atop a small ravine. All of this stage enjoys panoramic views north across lowland Craven to the Yorkshire Dales, coupled, in late summer, with the scent of heather wafting from the adjacent moorland.

The path runs on to the flat top of Weets Hill, remaining on the wallside over the brow. A path branches off past a sprawling cairn to the waiting Ordnance Survey column on the very summit. At 1302ft/397m Weets Hill not surprisingly offers a stunning view, which is further enhanced by the trig. point's location on the northern edge of the plateau. Barnoldswick is still in view as the trig. is touched, though the prospect north to the shapely pairing of Ingleborough and Penyghent is perhaps the highlight. To the west now Pendle Hill is revealed, with Longridge Fell behind and then the Bowland massif.

On Weets Hill, looking west to Pendle Hill

Another path returns to the wallside footpath to descend onto Gisburn Old Road at a gate off the hill. A short-lived green way runs on to the isolated Weets House. Gisburn Old Road was a major packhorse route prior to the construction of the turnpike below - the present A682 road. Northwards from here it runs a short, barely discernible section before resuming as Coal Pit Lane for the last stage to Gisburn.

Follow this quiet, cul-de-sac road for almost a mile past several houses. This leisurely stroll gives ample time to survey a wide sweep of East Lancashire, with Boulsworth Hill leading round to the moors above Burnley. Further right are Admergill and Burn Moor backed by Pendle Hill. **Shortly before the isolated Peel's House take a gate on the left. Head away on a new wallside track to the beginning of the walled green lane of Lister Well Road.** Down below are the Foulridge reservoirs, the nearer one being particularly extensive. Great Edge, Kelbrook Moor and Elslack Moor sit across the valley.

Lister Well Road provides a gem of a stroll alongside the rampant heather carpet of White Moor. This way rolls on for some time, gradually declining until commencing a more pronounced descent. Here, from a stile by a gate on the right, head off on another track down the heather moor. As it swings right to a pond, continue down to a gate below to leave the moor. Ahead is a hatful of West Craven settlements, including Barnoldswick, Salterforth, Earby, Kelbrook and Foulridge. **Descend the pasture to a gate/stile in the corner below, and an arrow-like green way descends to the farm at Copy Nook. Its drive continues downhill onto the B6251 Foulridge-Barnoldswick road, conveniently alongside the** *Fanny Grey* **pub.**

Just beyond the pub, a stile points down the field towards Booth House Farm. Don't go down into its yard, but use a gate on the left to cross a field bottom. From a gap-stile at the end cross a garden, passing left of the house and several others to emerge onto a road. Turn right down this for Salterforth, soon reaching the Leeds-Liverpool Canal and adjacent pub on the edge of the village. The *Anchor Inn* is a celebrated canalside pub (see WALK 10).

Join the canal towpath opposite the pub (left), and head away past colourful scenes at Salterforth Moorings. For more on the canal, see WALK 10. **The canal swings under the B6383 Barnoldswick-Kelbrook road at Park Bridge, and is followed to the next arched canal bridge, Cockshutt Bridge, alongside which is Lower Park Marina, with refreshments.** En route we pass the embankment and a forlorn stone abutment of the Barnoldswick branch line. Opened in 1871, it ran for less than two miles from a junction with the old Skipton-Colne railway. The line closed in 1965, a casualty of Dr. Beeching's infamous axe. **Remain on the towpath to the next bridge by the Silentnight bed factory. On climbing to the road, turn left along it, and as Rainhall Road it leads back to the town centre. At the traffic lights turn right to finish, or to see the attractive Town Square, keep straight on and then turn right down Ellis Street.**

14

LEEDS-LIVERPOOL CANAL

START *Greenberfield*   *Grid ref. SD 887481*

DISTANCE *5¼ miles*

ORDNANCE SURVEY MAPS
1:50,000
Landranger 103 - Blackburn & Burnley
1:25,000
Outdoor Leisure 21 - South Pennines

ACCESS *Start from the the British Waterways car park at Greenberfield Locks, just off the B6252 Barnoldswick-Thornton in Craven road. The main road is served by Skipton-Colne/Burnley buses.*

A leisurely, low level walk focusing on the many attractive features seen from the towpath, but also visiting two lovely old churches.

S   Greenberfield Locks are a set of three that lift the canal to its highest altitude. Though the canal opened in 1816, these locks replaced an earlier staircase a few years later: the old course is still partly evident to the right of the towpath on re-entering the site at the end of the walk. The lock-keeper's cottage still serves its original purpose, and features a sundial of 1824. Boaters' facilities and a refreshment kiosk with picnic area add to the colour and interest.

     Joining the towpath head left/north just as far as the road bridge after the first lock. Here join the road, cross the bridge and follow the road the short way to join the main road (B6252). The road here is on the line of the Roman road linking forts at Elslack (2 miles north-east) with Ribchester. **Bear left along this the short way to the Rolls-Royce factory. Just past a *Welcome to Barnoldswick* sign, look for a small kissing-gate nearly hidden on the right. A little path rises past Gill Hall.** Turn to look back at its lovely front with an array of mullioned windows. The house dates from the 16th century and was at one time the rectory. **Continue on the fieldside above the wooded**

cleft of The Gill, and at the top a stile admits into the churchyard of St. Mary le Gill. Pass round to the right to gain the front of the church and the gateway onto its access road.

St. Mary le Gill (or Ghyll) is a splendid old church with a large 16th century tower. The interior features a fine arrangement of box-pews and an awesome three-decker pulpit. The Cistercian monks who founded Kirkstall Abbey at Leeds had previously attempted, unsuccessfully, to settle here. Occasionally visitors can, at their own risk, ascend 50 spiral steps to the top of the tower, for an exposed view over the incredibly vast 500 year-old roof to the surrounding country-side. Also seen at close quarters are three great bells dated 1723. On summer weekends a tearoom often operates.

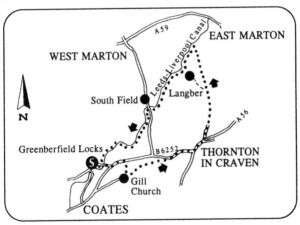

From the church gateway go left, down a narrow snicket between churchyard and cemetery. This descends to a slab crossing of the tiny stream and straight up onto the Ghyll golf course. Rise left of a small plantation and up again to a path through a narrow belt of trees to a kissing-gate out of the course. Rise away, skirting the grassy knoll and aiming for Thornton church tower straight ahead. This modest elevation gives sweeping views north to the Dales skyline. Cross an access track (to a mast) and a stile and on again, a stile at the end admitting onto the bank above the B6252. Go right, following the verge to a stile in the hedge directly opposite Thornton-in-Craven church. St. Mary's isolated church dates largely from the 15th century: note the mis-spelt inscription of 1510 on the tower.

Advance along the roadside footway to the village centre. Passed en route are a charming little row of five almshouses dated 1815. At the junction with the main road, note the village's Millennium Project, an attractive arrangement of seats and villagers tablets beneath a splendid clock. **Turn left on the main road through the village.** Thornton-in-Craven boasts an attractive arrangement of houses and gardens astride the Pennine Way. Unfortunately it is also astride the busy A56, and it sloping green, which features the village stocks, is rather devastated by the constant rumble of traffic.

Almost at the end, bear left along the cul-de-sac Cam Lane: note that this opening stage follows the Pennine Way as far as the canal. At some attractive cottages the road becomes unsurfaced, leading on past another house and out into the fields. The views ahead open out to embrace the Malhamdale Hills, with Flasby Fell to the right and Weets Hill and Pendle Hill around to the left. **The rough road runs on to Langber Farm, but it is left immediately after some modern farm buildings. From a gate on the right head up the field, and over the brow to a gate in the corner just below.** This reveals a lovely view of archetypal West Craven scenery, while more distantly,

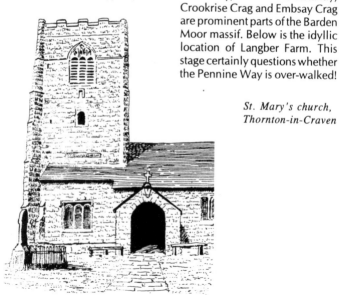

Crookrise Crag and Embsay Crag are prominent parts of the Barden Moor massif. Below is the idyllic location of Langber Farm. This stage certainly questions whether the Pennine Way is over-walked!

St. Mary's church,
Thornton-in-Craven

Drop down to the delectably gliding Langber Beck, which is crossed by a single stone slab in a lovely corner. Cross to a stile ahead, then slant right up the field to a stile at a fence junction on the brow of Langber Hill. This is another good viewpoint, featuring Flasby Fell, Crookrise Crag, Embsay Crag, Skipton Moor, Elslack Moor, and back round to Weets Hill and Pendle Hill. Just ahead, East Marton's church tower is prominent. **Continue to slant down the field to a hidden stile near the corner, then up to another to access the canal towpath just above.**

Turn left on the towpath, which is followed for 2½ tranquil miles back to the start. This is an uneventful and relaxing stroll through archetypal West Craven countryside, featuring grassy limestone knolls formed at the end of the last Ice Age. The canal undertakes some appreciable meandering to hold its contour round their flanks. **The only bridge encountered is South Field Bridge.** Beyond here the surroundings open out to reveal Gill church above the factory, soon joined by Thornton church back to the left. **The canal runs on to the county boundary near the factory. Rounding a couple more bends, a stone-arched bridge conveys the towpath to the other bank, just past which are Greenberfield Locks.**

St Mary le Gill

15

RAMSHAW

START Carleton   Grid ref. SD 972496

DISTANCE 4¾ miles

ORDNANCE SURVEY MAPS
1:50,000
Landranger 103 - Blackburn & Burnley
1:25,000
Outdoor Leisure 21 - South Pennines

ACCESS Start from the village centre, roadside parking. Buses from Skipton.

A pleasant contrast between wooded becks and open country.

S Northernmost of the South Pennine gritstone villages, Carleton looks across the Aire Gap to the Yorkshire Dales. Grouped around the large, 140-year old mill (newly converted to residential use) are the *Swan* pub, the church and a Post office/shop. **Head west on the Colne road past the mill, and just before the last house on the left, turn up a little street called The Wend. After a couple of short terraces it becomes a rough track, crossing Catlow Gill and swinging right to run parallel with it. Beyond a motley assortment of farm buildings it emerges much improved to run through several fields, with the tree-lined beck down to the right.**

 Fading at a pronounced bend in the beck, turn upstream on the rim of the steep-sided gill. Part-way up the field it is apparent we're now above a side beck, and a marker post sends a faint path slanting into the floor of the gill. Cross a stile and the stream, and a path winds up the opposite bank. Resume left atop the bank up to a wall-stile ahead. Looking back, the expanse of Barden Moor behind Skipton features Cracoe war memorial beyond Crookrise Crag, with Kirkby Fell and Fountains Fell the heights above Malham; Great Whernside soon fills the gap between shapely Flasby Fell and Barden Moor.

Slant right up a large field to a gate at the top, on the rim of Carleton Glen. Contour across and then down to the beck in a gap in the trees. Across, go a few yards up to a stile in a short length of wall. Climb away again and resume left above the bank, again to a wall-stile. From this aim up the field to Gawthorpe House, joining its drive at a stile. Turn left past the house, a track descending to cross a stream then rising to a gate. Bear right up to an old stile onto Park Lane. Turn up to a T-junction and go left, past a boundary stone and a lesser right fork, to arrive at Tewit Cote farm road. Go left on this, and as it drops towards the house bear left to a stile in the far corner.

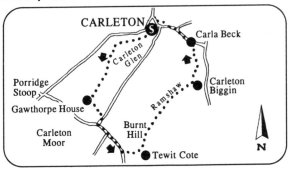

Entering the rough moorland of Burnt Hill, follow the wall on to a stile taking the path to the other side. In a slight dip beyond, a gate returns it to the west side, and the way resumes along the level moorland ridge of Ramshaw. This narrows to give airy views before reaching the abrupt start of the descent. This heathery crest is a delight, the views over Airedale extending to an array of Dales fells. Closer to hand are countless Airedale villages and landmarks. **Drop off the steep end and remain with the wall through several enclosures, by-passing Carleton Biggin to emerge via a gate onto its drive.**

Turn left down the drive, and with a road in sight, locate a stile in the adjacent wall and cross the field to a similar stile. From here descend to the sprawl of barns at Carla Beck Farm. Go left a little from a gate giving access, and turn right before the actual farm to find a stile emptying onto Carla Beck Lane. Turn left along the road to re-enter the village. At the point of re-entry is Spence's Court, 17th century almshouses with spinning galleries above a courtyard. **The finish can be varied by squeezing between the modern houses on the right, where a flagged path runs on to emerge by St. Mary's church.**

16

ELSLACK MOOR

START Elslack   Grid ref. SD 929492

DISTANCE 6½ miles

ORDNANCE SURVEY MAPS
1:50,000
Landranger 103 - Blackburn & Burnley
1:25,000
Outdoor Leisure 21 - South Pennines

ACCESS Start from the village centre. Parking on the wide verge of the Lothersdale road where it leaves the village. The nearby A56 is served by Skipton-Colne/Burnley buses.

A steady climb to a superb moortop with superlative views.

S   Elslack is a tiny community hidden just off the A56 Skipton-Colne road. The centre consists of a group of dignified dwellings around a miniscule green. The large *Tempest Arms* pub near the main road advertises the 'big' local family of nearby Broughton Hall. At Elslack the Romans had a fort on their road from Ribchester to Ilkley. **Leave the village by the Lothersdale road (Moor Lane), and at the first opportunity take a drive left to Smearber Farm. Entering the yard, go through the gate across and follow the wall away.**

Extensive plantations on the slopes above obscure the walk's moorland objective; while big views to the left look north to shapely Flasby Fell and greater Dales heights beyond. **When the wall parts company advance to a gate in the next wall. The route maintains this near-straight course through numerous fields towards a plantation ahead, each time with a well placed stile. Continue on with a fence, advancing to a gate in the wall ahead. From a stile at the end, go on again to a stile ahead, then several stiles trace the wall until there is no stile ahead. Here take a gate on the right onto the open moorland of Scarcliff.**

Follow the wall to a gate in it beyond the plantation. Note an unofficial short-cut remains on the moor, shadowing the wall up to Higher Scarcliff. **From the gate cross the field to join a farm road up towards Lower Scarcliff. Pass left of it and back onto the base of the moor. Turn right on the access track to the renovated Higher Scarcliff. Now rise gently left across the moor on a short-lived sunken path. After levelling out it falters, simply keep on to the wall ahead and bear left with it, down to meet the old Skipton-Colne road.** This moorland highway was once the major route linking the two towns, more direct and less hazardous than the valley route that ultimately replaced it.

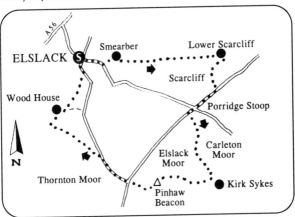

Turning right, the road climbs steeply between moors before levelling out to reach a crossroads at a plantation corner. Alongside is the 18th century guidepost of Porridge Stoop. It still bears the names of Settle, Skipton, Keighley and Colne, along with carved hands pointing the way. **Advance straight across, but before the cattle-grid take a stile onto a corner of Carleton Moor. A thin path shadows the wall rising gently up the heathery moor: when the wall turns, turn with it.** Pinhaw's top is now across to the right, but is forgotten for now as the top of Carleton Moor is traversed. Views ahead look to the Aire Valley beneath a Rombalds Moor skyline, with Earl Crag and its monuments directly ahead. **The grand path drops down to a corner stile off the moor. Turn right for one minute along the fieldtop, joining the Pennine Way at a stile back onto Elslack Moor.**

Once again a wall provides company, initially, before the PW breaks free and rises gradually to Pinhaw. Within 300 yards of the top a 'Keep to the PW' stone sees a grooved, grassy path double back to the right, its fading course running 130 yards down the slope to a small inscribed stone marked on the OS map. Robert Wilson died here in 1805, one of the guards who at this time still manned the beacon: men of three surrounding parishes shared the duties.

The broad path runs on to the Ordnance Survey column on Pinhaw. Despite a modest altitude of 1273ft/388m, Pinhaw is the highest point in the northernmost tract of the South Pennines. As a result it boasts an extensive 360° panorama, with the Yorkshire Dales fells to the north being the finest feature - keen eyes might pick out the limestone cliff of Malham Cove. Without its modern adornments of trig. point and cairn, the summit remains highly distinguishable as the raised site of a beacon (illustrated on page 79). This would have been one of a long chain that stretched across the country centuries ago, to warn of impending danger and also celebrate major events.

Two paths leave, but merge within 100 yards amid the heathery knolls of Elslack Moor. A wall is quickly joined to lead out onto the old Skipton-Colne road again. Cross straight over and down the moorland road opposite, amid some lovely tracts of heather. Looking across Thornton Moor over the wall, Barnoldswick sits beneath Weets Hill, which is overtopped by Pendle Hill. **Remain on the Pennine Way as it bears left, over a stile and down the moor alongside the wall. This smashing stride leads to a level, moister section with stone flags and duckboards. Eventually a corner stile exits the moor, a little below which a novel footbridge crosses stream and wall in tandem. Here leave the Pennine Way, and aim across the field to a gate above the farm buildings of Wood House.**

Follow the access road to the right, and half-way along the field take a stile in the wall to slant down to the next stile. Around this point Elslack appears below. **Head away with the left-hand wall, and after two further stiles leave the wall at a short row of grubbed trees to aim towards a farm. From a gate in a fence at the bottom of the hill, cross a field to a gate/stile onto the road just above the farm. Elslack is now just two minutes down the hill.**

Porridge Stoop

LOTHERSDALE HILLS

START *Lothersdale*   *Grid ref. SD 959459*

DISTANCE *5 miles*

ORDNANCE SURVEY MAPS
1:50,000
Landranger 103 - Blackburn & Burnley
1:25,000
Outdoor Leisure 21 - South Pennines

ACCESS *Start from the village centre. Roadside parking. Served by occasional buses from Skipton via Cross Hills.*

A rich variety of paths and green lanes up and down the not so humble hills watching over lovely Lothersdale.

S Lothersdale is a highly attractive village strung along a quiet back road, and is very much off the beaten track. Its seclusion among folds of the hills did not prevent the arrival of the mill age, and the surviving chimney is indeed often all that can be seen of the village. The church stands high and isolated on the road to the east, while other features - including an old limestone quarry where prehistoric bones have been unearthed - are found further west. The *Hare & Hounds* is handily placed.

From the pub head east along the main street, and at the foot of the hill, immediately over a beck, take a rough track to the left. Emerging from walls, a lovely path climbs a smashing tract of open moorland. This offers good views back over the village in its Lothers Dale setting. **At the top the walls converge again, and fifty yards after joining the access road of Tow Top Lane, leave by a stile on the right. Accompany the wall along the fieldside, bearing left at the end to a stile onto Babyhouse Lane.** A look at the adjacent gatepost reveals a recycled milepost with the town names inscribed (the same origin as the better known Porridge Stoop in WALK 16).

Turn right to a crossroads. This spell enjoys big views east beyond Cononley Lead Mine and the Gib to the moorland heights across the Aire Valley. **Turn right again for Lothersdale (already?!), and after the first field take a stile on the left, down to a gate into a field. Descend by the wall to a bottom corner stile above a wood, and cross to another just yards beyond it. Now traverse two field tops to Leys House.** This stage enjoys views south to Earl Crag and its two monuments, with the massive boulder of the Hitching Stone on the skyline further back. **The garden is entered by a stile just down the wall, emerging between the houses onto an access road.**

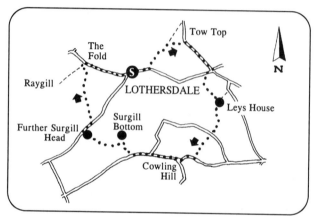

Turn down to the right on a splendid green lane to a footbridge and ford on Leys Beck, then steeply up the other side onto a road. The beck crossing is a grand spot, while the profusion of hollies enclosing the path is an indication of its age. **Cross straight over and up again to eventually meet a higher road, Long Lane: this sustained climb is initially narrow but opens out into a farm track.** Looking back across the side valley, the impressive facade of the big house at Stone Gappe is unmistakeable. Here, briefly, Charlotte Brontë was governess, and it became the Gateshead Hall of her novel *Jane Eyre*.

Turn right up Long Lane to Cowling Hill. With a graveyard in the trees, this exposed farming hamlet was once an appreciably larger settlement astride a once important road. Though its pub is long gone, a surprising survivor is a Baptist church secreted among farm buildings. **Continue up the road climbing steadily away, past a side road**

(its only sign being for the Pennine Way!) to ultimately level out. Having reached its summit, take the first farm road on the right. The actual path cuts a corner of the track at the end, through a small gate to the brow just beyond, overlooking the side valley of Surgill. This high point of the walk is a fine moment, with the moorland of Pinhaw behind this colourful little dale, while across to the right can be seen Lothersdale church, and a more distant Skipton Moor beyond.

The route drops down to rejoin the track, the sooner the better, given the extreme steepness of the slope. At the hairpin where it doubles back to the farm at Surgill Bottom, take a small gate by the gate just in front, and descend the fieldside to a corner stile. Slant down into the small wooded clough on a good little path that briefly forms. Across, it winds back out then slant up the field towards Further Surgill Head. At the wall/fence corner pass through two gates and along the fieldside to the houses, then follow the drive left up onto Hawshaw Road.

Turn briefly downhill, but before the farm at Near Surgill Head take a wall-stile on the left. Drop down a reedy corner to a very slender gap-stile, then down the field below to a stile midway along the wall. Resume the slant down to the bottom corner, and from the gate there down a small enclosure. At the bottom enter a short-lived enclosed grassy way. Emerging, the old sunken way slants down the right edge of the field, though the map suggests striking straight down to the bridge below. Just across it the track emerges into a field, rising to a stile/gate onto a rough road. Turn right to the road at The Fold, and then right along the length of the village to the start.

The Hare & Hounds, Lothersdale

18

PINHAW BEACON

START *Lothersdale*   *Grid ref. SD 959459*

DISTANCE *3 miles*

ORDNANCE SURVEY MAPS
1:50,000
Landranger 103 - Blackburn & Burnley
1:25,000
Outdoor Leisure 21 - South Pennines

ACCESS *Start from the village centre. Roadside parking. Served by occasional buses from Skipton via Cross Hills.*

A short and easy route onto a popular local moorland landmark.

S For a brief note on Lothersdale, please see page 75. **From the Hare & Hounds pub head east along the main street for a matter of yards, and take the Pennine Way where it is signed up through a farmyard. It climbs an enclosed track to emerge into a field. Ascend the wallside with a wooded sidestream over to the right, all the way up to a stile at the top corner. Go left up the field to a stile/gate onto a road. Cross straight over and up the Hewitts farm road. When it goes left keep straight up an enclosed grassy way into a field, then up the wallside to a stile onto a corner of Elslack Moor.**

A well worn path remains with the left-hand wall until breaking free to rise gradually to Pinhaw. Within 300 yards of the top a grassy path doubles back to visit Robert Wilson's Grave: see page 74. **The broad path runs on to reach the waiting Ordnance Survey column on Pinhaw, at 1273ft/388m. For a note on Pinhaw please see page 74. Two paths leave, but merge within 100 yards amid the heathery knolls of Elslack Moor. A wall corner is quickly reached, and here the PW is finally left.** If the ground is particularly wet, an unofficial short-cut sees a thin path cross directly to the stile off the moor, leaving the main path just beneath the aforementioned heathery knolls. **Go left with the moorside wall, and beyond a small marsh, a good little path runs over the brow.** This gives a fine view ahead over the dale, with the old limestone quarry at Raygill prominent, along with parts of the scattered village with the mill chimney conspicuous as ever. **The path curves left above a wall corner and along to a solid stile off the moor. Bear left, down past a wood corner and across a sizeable pasture to a gate/stile at the bottom. Descend the wallside to a stile onto a drive at Calf Edge Farm.**

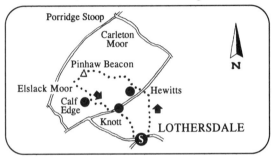

Go left on this drive which runs on and down onto a back road. Go left for two minutes, and over a stream turn right down a short driveway to Knott Farm. This splendid house boasts mullioned windows and a 1695 datestone. **Go straight on down a short track in front of the house, then from the left-hand gate a grassy track runs on between wall and fence. At the end it swings right to a gate in the corner. Head straight down the wallside, with the millpond in the village waiting below. At the bottom corner ignore the gate in favour of a wall-stile in front. Drop down to another stile, and a small bridge over the outflow onto the road in the village.** The old dam is a charming spot regularly frequented by swans and geese.

Pinhaw Beacon, looking to Pendle Hill

EARL CRAG

START Cowling   Grid ref. SD 967430

DISTANCE 6 miles

ORDNANCE SURVEY MAPS
1:50,000
Landranger 103 - Blackburn & Burnley
1:25,000
Outdoor Leisure 21 - South Pennines

ACCESS Start from Cowling parish church at Ickornshaw. This is at the western end of the village, just off the A6068. Roadside parking. Keighley-Colne buses run on the main road.

Lovely beck scenery contrasts with the main features of the walk, which provide breathtaking views of South Craven.

S Cowling is a windswept gritstone mill community, indeed a classic Pennine example. Its rows of dark terraces are strung along the length of the village, on or close to the main road over to Lancashire. The *Bay Horse* is Cowling's centrally placed pub, and there are several main street shops. The 19th century Holy Trinity church stands aloof, with a former Sunday School by the church gate. Nearby is the house where famous son Philip Snowden, an early 20th century Chancellor of the Exchequer, was born.

From the church gate take the road opposite, through the hamlet of Ickornshaw. After crossing Ickornshaw Beck, a stile on the left sends a part-flagged path climbing steeply to the main road. The *Black Bull* pub is just along to the right. **Go left briefly, and cross to a stile opposite. Ascend the field to Lower Summer House, using a stile to the left of the farm onto an access track. Rise briefly to a stile onto the foot of a walled green way rising above the farm.** Cowling Pinnacle perches on the edge of Earl Crag over to the left, while Pendle Hill appears far to the west. **Merging into Lumb Lane, advance**

straight on as far as a gate/stile. Though the route doesn't pass through, it is worth doing so to see a little waterfall at close hand on Lumb Head Beck.

The onward route takes a gate on the left, from where a part sunken way descends Wool Hey Brow by the wall. The big view ahead looks over this side valley of Dean Hole Clough to the Pinnacle, with extensive moorland slopes to the right. At the bottom Lumb Head Beck is crossed and the path runs on through trees to a gate in front of the main beck. An old wooden farm bridge sits just upstream. Across, the walled green way of Close Lane scales the opposite slope. Initially moist, it quickly improves to emerge onto the sharp bend of a narrow road at Deanfield.

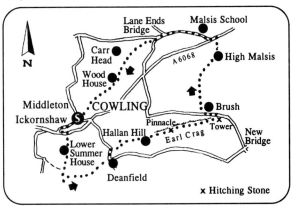

While the quickest way to Wainman's Pinnacle is straight up Piper Lane, turn left on this bend, just as far as Court House Farm on the right. Enter the yard and pass the house out into the field behind. Follow the wall away to the very end, where a stile above a small wooded clough admits onto a broad green way. Go left just thirty yards to its tapering demise at a stile. Through this, climb the steep bank on the right. The Cowling scene is well presented below, with the entire village laid out end to end. The slope eases to reveal Wainman's Pinnacle in front, beyond the farm at Hallan Hill.

Advance straight up the fields with the wall on the right. At the farm keep left of the buildings to follow the drive out through a gate. Emerging onto the open moor of Cludders, bear left towards the distinct edge, being aware that an old quarry rim makes it all too distinct. To the south is a big sweep of moorland, looking to the Hitching Stone above Stott Hill Moor and Ickornshaw Moor. **A broad old way surmounts the quarried edge and now rises gently up above the broken gritstone outcrops to the waiting Pinnacle.**

Earl Crag is a mile-long gritstone outcrop which dominates the skyline of South Craven. Atop it, but a long half-mile apart, are its two permanent occupants, and it is only at this point that Lund's Tower is revealed at the far end. Built on solid rock, the Pinnacle dates from the early 19th century and is better known as Cowling Pinnacle. The panorama is both extensive and absorbing: many of the more local features draw the eye beyond the rim of the outcrops, including Farnhill Moor, Pinhaw Beacon, Skipton Moor, Rombalds Moor, and Airedale villages such as Cross Hills, Bradley and Kildwick.

Rough moorland walking is demanded for a detour of a good 1½ miles to visit the Hitching Stone: this simply follows the wall south from the Pinnacle, across Piper Lane and along the moorside to rise to the monstrous boulder, which can be surmounted.

At the Hitching Stone, looking back to the Pinnacle

The promenade along the crest of Earl Crag to the beckoning Lund's Tower is a local favourite, and is as obvious as it looks, crossing a couple of sturdy wall-stiles and finally a fence-stile en route. Built by James Lund and known locally as Cowling Tower or Sutton Pinnacle, its grassy sward is set back from an old quarry. It boasts 39 spiral steps up to a small platform from which to survey the exhilarating vista extending far into the Yorkshire Dales. The drop of the quarry exaggerates the airiness: not for the faint-hearted!

Leave the tower by a path from the fence, which circumvents the cliff on concrete steps to drop down onto a road. Turn down this just as far as a drive to Brush on the right. Earl Crag now presents a jagged skyline just above. **Ignoring the drive, descend half-left to a gate, below which is a short enclosed way. At the end simply follow the wall down through a succession of fields, eventually reaching a gate from where the wall and route swing right, a track materialising to arrive at High Malsis. Don't enter the farmyard but take a gate/ stile just below to reach a short row of houses. Here an access road descends to the A6068.** The *Dog & Gun* pub, with its splendid freestanding sign, is just two minutes along to the right. Over the road stands Malsis, a large house that is now a school in extensive grounds.

Cross to the footway opposite and go left beneath horse chestnuts to the junction. Take the side road (Carr Head Lane) for a leisurely ten minutes, over Lumb Mill Bridge and passing Lumb Mill House and Lumb Mill Farm. The big skyline to the left features the crest of Earl Crag, dead level between its two monuments. **Just beyond a branch right, take one to the left to descend to Lane Ends Bridge. Immediately over it, re-cross Lumb Mill Beck on a footbridge and head upstream. The sizeable beck can submerge the first section of path, making a detour above the wooded bank necessary from a flight of stones steps above the bridge.** These initial stages are particularly delightful, passing a well preserved limekiln in the parklike surroundings of Carr Head Hall (seen early on, up to the right).

Past the confluence of Ickornshaw Beck and Gill Beck is a high footbridge (Ridge Mill Bridge) on the latter, across which follow a path away from the beck. This broadens to a track junction just around the corner beneath isolated Wood House: bear right along the pleasant green byway of Cinder Hill Lane. This leads unerringly back - high above Ickornshaw Beck - to broaden into a firm track at a barnyard, ultimately emerging by the church.

*On Earl Crag:
Lund's Tower (right),
Wainman's Pinnacle*

20

SUTTON CLOUGH

START Sutton-in-Craven   *Grid ref. SE 005441*

DISTANCE 4½ miles

ORDNANCE SURVEY MAPS
1:50,000
Landranger 104 - Leeds, Bradford & Harrogate
1:25,000
Outdoor Leisure 21 - South Pennines

ACCESS Start from the village centre. Roadside parking. Served by
Keighley-Skipton buses.

*Colourful surroundings and steep slopes, with excellent views over
and beyond mid-Airedale. The central feature is the hugely attractive,
deep-cut wooded dell of Sutton Clough.*

S Sutton-in-Craven (locally just Sutton, as it's a long way to the
next Sutton) is a sizeable village in the shadow of steep hills to the
south. It is dominated by its large mill buildings, and the older High
Street area has some fine old cottages. The public park, three pubs,
several shops and a chip shop add further benefits. **From the main
junction outside the park and the *Black Bull*, follow the High Street
(signed to Laycock). Keep left to a fork just before the beck, and here
take the unsigned road straight ahead. This is Hall Drive, which runs
on as a suburban street beyond an impressive arch, a double Lodge,
East and West. Beyond the houses a footbridge takes the ensuing
broad way into the trees of Sutton Clough.**
**Keep on the main way, passing arched bridge, footbridge and
concrete bridge before succumbing to a small footbridge. A good
path traces the opposite bank, and just above a beautiful confluence
the climbing begins. Enjoy some lovely waterplay as the path climbs
between massive boulders.** A particularly enormous boulder hangs
above the very steep slope opposite. **The path remains near the beck**

in its wooded ravine until it turns to climb steeply away. **Here leave it, and advance a few yards to the streamside before crossing to the opposite bank. A few yards further upstream, a good path doubles back up the slope to the left. This slants up to a stile out of the clough.**

Turn right up the field towards the house above. From a stile to its left, advance to find a ladder-stile behind a stone outhouse. Descend the wallside to a stream, where a stile on the left accesses its beech wooded environs. An attractive little fall tumbles over a rocky ledge immediately below. **Within fifty yards a less obvious, part-stepped path drops down to cross the beck, and on a short way to a stile out. Contour round the sloping field behind to find a splendid stile with steps down the other side.** This is a pleasant corner above the limits of another branch of the wooded clough. **Slant up through rampant hollies to find a stile at the top, then shadow the wallside up to two neighbouring stiles onto a surfaced farm road. Go left out through the farm and out onto a road known as Ellers.**

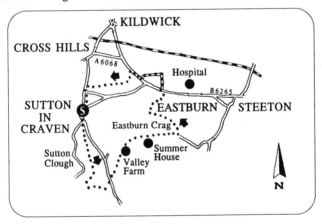

Cross straight over to Long House, behind which a very brief walled way leads out into a field. There are views back up to Cowling Tower on Earl Crag, high above Cowling's side valley. **Cross the field to a gate, and aiming for Valley Farm ahead, pass beneath a tiny stone hut to a stile in the facing wall. Advance through bracken to a wall corner stile, then go left to a gate into the yard at Valley Farm. Pass straight through and out via a gate onto a short-lived walled way. Advance to the field end where a communications mast stands**

near the North Yorkshire-West Yorkshire boundary wall. From the stile, cross to a gate into a sliver of woodland, and quickly out the other side. **Head on through an old gateway/gap then bear right to a gate onto Summer House's drive.** The section from the wood is a diversion not shown on current maps.

Head away on the long drive out. Just before a bend where it becomes surfaced (Intake Lane), take a gate on the left from where a grassy track drops away. Fine views up the valley are enjoyed, featuring Cross Hills, Kildwick, Farnhill Moor, Flasby Fell and into the heart of the Dales. Immediately to the left of the path is the modest bouldery edge of Eastburn Crag. **A short enclosed section leads down to the colourful country around Eastburn's old quarry. The grand path slants down well above the quarry, and as it curves down the side, a short-cut path drops more directly down.**

The track becomes an access road, dropping below the quarry environs to enter Eastburn as the paved Moor Lane. Eastburn is a tiny village that sprang to prominence when the large Airedale Hospital was built between here and neighbouring Steeton. Eastburn's more recent by-passing has certainly not left the place a backwater on the old road. Its pub is the *White Bear*, just further along to the left.

The village is entered by the Post office and a chippy. Take advantage of a pedestrian crossing over the main road (B6265), then go left a few yards to escape down Green Lane. At the bottom turn left along Lyon Road to rejoin the main road. Cross and go right, leaving by a surfaced path immediately after crossing Holme Beck at Eastburn Bridge. This firm path shadows the beck upstream all the way back to Sutton. On rejoining the road, turn left and conclude through the pleasant surroundings of the public park.

Earl Crag from Eastburn Bridge

The stocks, Sutton Park

21

CONONLEY LEAD MINE

START Cononley   Grid ref. SD 989469

DISTANCE 4¾ miles

ORDNANCE SURVEY MAPS
1:50,000
Landranger 103 - Blackburn & Burnley
1:25,000
Outdoor Leisure 21 - South Pennines

ACCESS Start from the village centre. Car park where Meadow Lane
meets the Main Street, also roadside parking. Served by Keighley-
Skipton buses and trains.

*A simple circuit of Cononley's own little hill, with the unique
attraction of a preserved lead mine and superb views both up and
down the Aire Valley.*

S   Cononley is a traditional Airedale mill village. Its centre hides
many attractive old cottages and two pubs. **From the bridge by the
Post office walk up Main Street past the *New Inn*, and leave by an
access road along the near side of the Institute. It climbs steeply
towards Town Head Farm, but is left at the sharp bend just before
it, instead continuing straight up a walled green way. At the top turn
right to accompany a gradually rising wall on an improving grassy
track.** Looking back, there are good views back over the village and
up the Aire Valley into the Dales.
      **The way runs steadily along to a couple of houses at Great Gib
and Little Gib.** At this very early stage in the walk, virtually all its
climbing is over! **Advance straight on their access road, which
quickly swings right to pass the waiting Cononley Lead Mine.** Unique
in this book are the restored workings of this lead mine, dominated by
a chimney and a Cornish-style engine house. These imposing remains
of Yorkshire's southernmost lead mine are curiously isolated from the

contrastingly extensive workings at Grassington Moor above Wharfedale. Long part of the Duke of Devonshire's vast lands, the site was restored by the indefatigable Earby Mines Research Group, who run a fascinating Museum of Yorkshire Dales Lead Mining at nearby Earby. The Grade II listed buildings date from around 1842, as does the reservoir just across the access road. Mining at Cononley ceased in 1882, though the spoil was worked for barytes during the 20th century.

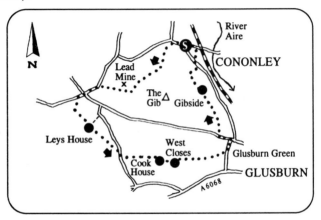

Returning to the access road, this leads out onto a through road. Go left to a crossroads, and straight over on the Lothersdale road. After the first field take a stile on the left, down to a gate into a field. Descend by the wall to a bottom corner stile above a wood, and cross to another just yards beyond it. Now traverse two field tops to Leys House. This stage enjoys views south to Earl Crag and its two monuments. **The garden is entered by a stile just down the wall, emerging between the houses onto an access road. From the stile in front resume as before, across a couple of steep fieldtops towards a farm ahead. Advance to the gate just above it, beneath which a hidden stile leads onto Leys Lane.**

Drop down just past the farm to a stile on the left. Head off along the wallside through several fields. The Earl Crag skyline remains dominant over to the right. **Entering the field just in front of Cook House, don't advance to it but immediately take a stile on the right. Pass to the right of the farm buildings to a stile in front of the**

house, and continue straight on to a gate/stile just in front. **Cross the fieldtop to a stile just short of the corner, then slant down the next field to the houses at West Closes. Turn left along the access road, which leads past several farms to ultimately emerge onto Green Lane at Glusburn Green.**

Go left past some desirable residences to the Lothersdale road, and left on this. Just before Well Spring Farm, a stile/gate on the right send a wallside track away. At the end take a kissing-gate and on past an old concrete reservoir to emerge into the open on a super green way. Extensive views see the Aire Valley stretch for miles in both directions. Across it are Rombalds, Farnhill and Skipton Moors, while behind Skipton itself rise the shapely tops of Flasby Fell, and also Barden Moor. Villages on show include Bradley, Farnhill, Cross Hills and our own objective.

The path runs on though an old stile and slants down to a gate to merge into a track on a hairpin bend. This angles gently down through a large bracken pasture to meet a wall. Cross over a farm track above Gibside and on above a poultry farm at the end. A gate accesses a chicken run, beneath which descend a tapering field. A choice of stiles lead onto Windle Lane, and down onto the road on the edge of the village. Go left past the terrace of Aire View. This amazingly long terrace is known to some as Frying Pan Row, as at one time the occupants had but one such pan to share, this being in the ownership of the local poacher! **Immediately after Aire View take an urban path down past sports fields to emerge onto the road in front of the *Railway* pub. Go left for the village centre, or right for the railway station.**

Cononley Lead Mine

22

RIVER AIRE

START Kildwick   Grid ref. SE 010458

FINISH Skipton   Grid ref. SD 983513

DISTANCE 5¾ miles

ORDNANCE SURVEY MAPS
1:50,000
Landranger 103 - Blackburn & Burnley
Landranger 104 - Leeds, Bradford & Harrogate
1:25,000
Outdoor Leisure 21 - South Pennines

ACCESS Start from the corner by pub and church. Parking nearby, on the old road. This is a linear walk making use of the regular Keighley-Kildwick-Skipton bus service. It should also be possible to use the rail line when the anticipated Cross Hills station re-opens.

A low level, linear walk tracing the course of the river Aire.

S   Only since the mid-1980s has Kildwick sat happily back from the bustle of the A629 through the Aire Valley. Church, pub, cottages and bridge combine to create a delightful picture. The bridge is one of the oldest on the Aire, having been rebuilt by the Canons of Bolton in 1305. Since widened, gaze from the upstream parapets to see two of the arches pointed, the other two rounded. The *White Lion* pub overlooks it. St. Andrew's church - known as the 'Lang (long) Kirk o'Craven' - is a beautiful old building, with an imposing tower and a lovely low-slung roof. Within is much carved oak, and fragmentary remains of 10th century Anglo-Saxon crosses (two of which bear figures). Note also the resplendent Sir Robert de Styverton monument of 1307. Stiveton was the old name for Steeton, the village just down the valley. Alongside the church is the old schoolhouse of 1839. The Leeds-Liverpool Canal runs immediately behind.

Cross Kildwick Bridge to find an underpass beneath the A629 Skipton road to the right of the roundabout, joining Station Road (B6172) to head off into suburban Cross Hills. After bridging the railway, a stile immediately before a filling station sends a short snicket along to emerge into a field. Landmarks in this open view include Farnhill Pinnacle on its pocket moorland to the right, and shapely Flasby Fell further up the dale.

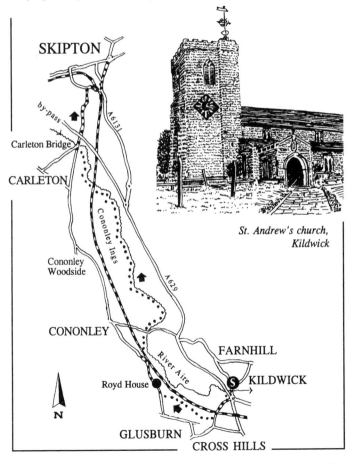

*St. Andrew's church,
Kildwick*

Bear left on a thin fieldside path to rise to a couple of stiles onto a rough access road. Don't follow it up to the road above, but slant back down another path to a small gate below, and on through a short enclosed way to re-emerge into open fields. The way runs on through stiles in several field centres, at the end accompanying a wall along to a stile onto the Cross Hills-Cononley road. Across the valley, Farnhill Hall is well seen on its knoll beneath Farnhill Moor.

Turn right, passing Royd House. Behind the gateway arch note the mullioned and transomed windows surviving from an earlier house, now merely a short section of wall. **Approaching the edge of Cononley, take stiles across the parallel railway and a riverside path runs upstream to Cononley Bridge.** Cononley is a traditional Airedale mill village. Its centre hides many attractive old cottages and two pubs, the *New Inn* and the *Railway*. It also has a station, though its level crossing causes the main road to be closed longer than it is open!

Cross the road, not the bridge, and a stile sends a path upstream. There now follows an extended riverbank ramble that adheres tightly to the silently gliding Aire for virtually three miles around the innumerable twists and turns of Cononley Ings. Across the valley above Bradley rise the slopes of the Standard, while ahead, the much vaster girth of Barden Moor rises alongside Flasby Fell beyond Skipton: Crookrise Crag and Embsay Crag are its prominent features. **This truly delightful walk finally ends at Carleton Bridge. A stile accesses the road by the bridge, which is crossed to follow the footway along Carleton Road into Skipton. The quickest way to the bus station bears right onto the main road, then turning left. For the rail station, go left on Carleton New Road, joining Broughton Road (A6069) opposite the station.**

Skipton is derived from 'sheep-town', for wool has played an important role for many centuries. This capital of Craven occupies a strategic location in the Aire Gap, owing, to this day, as much allegiance to East Lancashire as the West Riding of Yorkshire. The broad High Street, with its spacious setts up either side, is an animated scene on market days (Monday, Wednesday, Friday, Saturday), when a variety of stalls squeeze cheek by jowl in front of the shops. At the head of the street stands the parish church, dating in part from the 14th century. Of special note are a rood screen of 1533, the great oak beams of the medieval roof, and the Clifford tombs. Around the altar are those of Henry, 1st Earl of Cumberland (1542) and his wife Margaret, each superbly depicted on brass; and the tomb of the Third Earl (1605), richly decorated with Clifford armorial bearings.

Skipton's finest building is its well preserved castle. Its first greeting is an enormous early 14th century gatehouse with rounded towers: it was restored by the indomitable Lady Anne Clifford, and the motto *Desormais* - henceforth - is her work. Inside is a spacious green and the castle proper. A feature of particular interest is the cramped conduit court, in the centre of which grows a renowned yew tree.

The castle dates from Norman times, coming into the Cliffords' possession in 1309, when it was largely rebuilt. For 3½ centuries it was the home of the powerful Cliffords. Henry the 10th (Shepherd) Lord spent his youth in anonymity in the company of monks and shepherds before being returned after the Battle of Bosworth in 1485; George, 13th Lord and Third Earl, was a sea captain who helped thwart the Armada; while his remarkable daughter Anne, last of the Cliffords, still journeyed between her various castles - including Brougham and Appleby, in Westmorland - at a ripe old age to restore and maintain them.

A short excursion around the back of the castle, by crossing Mill Bridge over Eller Beck, leads by way of three parallel watercourses - the beck, the Springs Branch of the canal (down which quarried stone was brought), and a mill-cut - to view the impregnable northern face of the castle. From this central location, Skipton Woods extend up behind the town. Also worth visiting is the Craven Museum, while the Leeds-Liverpool Canal glides through the heart of town.

The Gatehouse, Skipton Castle

93

LOG OF THE WALKS

WALK	DATE	NOTES
1		
2		
3		
4		
5		
6		
7		
8		
9		
10		
11		
12		
13		
14		
15		
16		
17		
18		
19		
20		
21		
22		

SOME USEFUL ADDRESSES

Ramblers' Association
2nd Floor, Camelford House, 87-89 Albert Embankment, London SE1 7BR
Tel. 020-7339 8500

Information Centres
Tourist Information Centre, 2-4 West Lane **Haworth**
    Tel. 01535-642329
Tourist Information Centre, Fernlea Avenue **Barnoldswick**
    Tel. 01282-666704
Tourist Information Centre, City Hall, Centenary Square **Bradford**
    Tel. 01274-753678
Tourist Information Centre, 35 Coach Street **Skipton**
    Tel. 01756-792809
Tourist Information Centre, Pendle Heritage Centre **Barrowford**
    Tel. 01282-661701
Wycoller Country Park **Wycoller** Tel. 01282-870253

Yorkshire Tourist Board
312 Tadcaster Road, York YO2 2HF Tel. 01904-707961

North West Tourist Board
Swan House, Swan Meadow Road, Wigan Pier, Wigan WN3 5BB
Tel. 01942-821222

Rights of Way/Countryside Officers
The walks in this book fall within three areas:
Bradford *(West Yorkshire)* Tel. 01274-435681
Craven *(North Yorkshire)* Tel. 01756-793344
Pendle *(Lancashire)* Tel. 01282-661930

Public Transport
West Yorkshire   Tel. 0113-245 7676
North Yorkshire   Tel. 0870-608 2608
Pendle   Tel. 01282-698533
National Rail Enquiry Line Tel. 08457-484950

Keighley & Worth Valley Railway   Tel. 01535-645214
    24-hour Timetable/Information Service: 01535-647777

Brontë Parsonage, Haworth   Tel. 01535-642323

INDEX

Principal features (walk number refers)